Paul ⟋⟋⟋⟋⟋ the 2014
Gordon Burn Prize and the *Bookseller* Book of the Year
Award, as well as being longlisted for the Man Booker
Prize, the Folio Prize and the Desmond Elliot Prize, and
shortlisted for the RSL Encore Award 2017.

Kingsnorth is also the author of the non-fiction books *One
No, Many Yeses, Real England, Confessions of a Recovering
Environmentalist* and *Savage Gods*, as well as two poetry col-
lections, *Kidland* and *Songs from the Blue River*. Kingsnorth
is the co-founder of The Dark Mountain Project.

Further praise for *Alexandria*:

'In this highly inventive trilogy, spanning 2,000 years,
Kingsnorth traces a line between the past and the future of
humanity, the tremendous upheaval we have experienced, and
that which may yet be to come.' *Times Literary Supplement*

'A passionately argued, often furious diatribe against the
human irresponsibility that has helped to trigger the crisis
of our present moment . . . Kingsnorth's greatest strength
lies, as ever, in the power and vision of his landscape writing.'
Guardian

'Wonderfully sharp and vivid . . . imaginatively conceived
and ecologically switched-on.' *The Spectator*

'A linguistic delight . . . Kingsnorth's novel is both of time
and out of time, and it posits some of the most urgent
questions of this millennium: where are we going, and
what will become of us.' *Financial Times*

'There's wisdom here, adventure, mystery and poetry.' *Daily Mail*

'England's greatest living writer ... Kingsnorth has finally travelled beyond literature into myth, cementing his title as a profoundly religious writer of uniquely English stamp.' *Washington Examiner*

'Kingsnorth writes from the very core of the agony and inner turmoil of being human in a living world dying at human hands ... *Alexandria* is a fervently proffered modern myth, offering no simple answers but plenty of meaning.' *Literary Hub*

'Unconventional orthography ... and mythical style add texture to a story that examines whether the body is essential or merely the mind's cage and whether humans are inherently destructive. When one stalker has doubts about his mission, his crisis of belief drives the book into unexpected territory.' *New Yorker*

---

by the same author

fiction
THE WAKE
BEAST

non-fiction
ONE NO, MANY YESES
REAL ENGLAND
CONFESSIONS OF A RECOVERING ENVIRONMENTALIST
SAVAGE GODS

poetry
KIDLAND AND OTHER POEMS
SONGS FROM THE BLUE RIVER

PAUL KINGSNORTH

ALEXANDRIA

FABER & FABER

First published in 2020
by Faber & Faber Ltd
Bloomsbury House
74–77 Great Russell Street
London WC1B 3DA

This paperback edition first published in 2022

Typeset by Faber & Faber Ltd
Printed in the UK by CPI Group (UK) Ltd, Croydon, CR0 4YY

A CIP record for this book
is available from the British Library

ISBN 978–0–571–32212–1

2 4 6 8 10 9 7 5 3 1

I was still in the womb when I dreamed this singing. It was given me by the Ravens. Now I am a man but have not forgotten it. I dreamed it before I ever was born. If I had been born when I dreamed it, I would have forgotten it. No, I did not learn it from other Mohaves, and I did not hear any of them sing it. In fact, no one else sings like this, for it was I that dreamed it myself.

Pamich, Mohave poet, 1903

Hwaet synt nu þæs foremeran þæs wisan goldsmiðes ban Welondes?

Boethius, *De Consolatione Philosophiae,*
Old English translation, c.900

i remember circle at me first blood, ah. then i was young.

there were more of us then, seven womyn, all circled in
fenn nekid and needeep in blak Water.

mother comin to me and i in centre of them all, and
shivered.

it is time between Dog and Wulf and Sky is closin over.
mother comin from Land where fyr is lighted and sayin
then to me and to womyn:

look up, see. She comes.

across eye blu Sky, wide like Sea, comes now great dark
shape, roilin bank of blak storm cloud movin steady over.
and Land growin dark and Waters and me legs in Waters
cold now, and i can not feel me feet.

mother holds me now nekid in Water, she has one hand
over me hart and one hand on me bak, and it seems cord
joins both her hands through me body.

then mother callin to Sky where dark now is rollin above
us like great wave and Birds fallin still.

Lady, she calls. great Lady wite Lady green Lady. great mother who is called Bree is called Erce is called Dine is called Maeri. enter in to body of this girl, take her blood and make her woman.

and circle callin, make her woman!

and womyn now closin in on me, womyn comin to me closin circle runnin hands softly over me body, sniffin me all over me body, smellin now scent of woman.

and dark bank of cloud then darkness, above now movin like storm wave, sudden becomin darkness in me. and now me body me lungs limbs soul mind is filled with some great risin colour and some great fallin dark, and where they meet is where mothers hands joinin through me very hart with cord of green that now is spiral, is gyre, windin through and bindin me to darkness above to ground below to all that was and will be to Clay to Birds to Greenrok to me body, womans body now, and to wild wite Lady of all Erth.

and i am Erth now, i am all things and and

and me nees shake and i can not feel me feet and me blood is runnin down me legs and in to cold cold Water.

and i cry then in some voice that is not mine, i cry, *terror! terror! o mother mother what is this i am afeart!*

and mother then she takes me in her arms she embraces
me, she holds me then like true mother, and i am soft in
her arms, she holds me above Waters so i do not fall and in
to me ear, gentle like blossom, she whispers:

you should be.

SIKKEL MOON

at moorin post she opens her robe and takes me right hand and placin it on her breast.

she held it there and lookin in me eyes, and her face is open like Sea.

i want to remember, she says.

and then: *you are so cold.*

its hard to keep standin with softness and warmth of her, with all hardness and softness of her in me one hand and through me.

come with me, i say. *come!*

she smiled. some times face she wears for others softens and dissolves and underneath is some unruined thing, some child no longer sharp against all edges.

keep your hand there, she said. *just keep it.*

he will not find us, i say, *he doesnt know.*

why are you so cold, she asked. *it is warm night.*

you will grow old, i said then. i was burnin, me body fyr. *your skin will be wite and hang like vines in holt, every thing will hang down, you will be pulled bak to Clay!*

ah, she says, *stop*.

there will be deth patches on me hands, i say, *me hair will come out, you will be crippled, dried, barren. all shame of deth, all of your beauty. we could go!*

i love you, i said, and words bring out unruined thing in her like Birds bring out Sun.

he wont know, i said, *it is not far, i know way. he wont follow.*

she held me hand, still on her breast.

just stand, she said. *just touch me.*

Bak then
Land was Land
Sea was Sea
There was no meetin

No meetin

Wite Cloud come between them
Blak Lightnin come between them
None could pass through

Bak then
No thing moved on Land
No thing moved in Sea
Only in Sky was life
In Sky moved Birds
First of all things

Cumrant watched from Greenrok
Cumrant waited for Blak Lightnin
When it broke
He flew

He flew

Through Wite Cloud

He flew
From Sea to Land
He flew

Hearin sound Sea made
As she longs for Land
Hearin sound Land made
As he longs for Sea

He come down

Bak then
Land awoke

What is this? cries Rook
Deoful said Cro
Grendel says Morrun
Beast said Robyn
Brother says Hern

Hern flyin with Cumrant
Bak through Wite Cloud to Sea
Hearin sound Sea made as she longs for Land

It is so he said

It is so

he told me he loved me and his words burnin, and his eyes burnt also and he puts his hand on me, over me hart.

i held his hand on me and he said he loved me but it was not me he loved, it was this moment of lovin. he loves what burns, his world is shaped from his seein of it, all his world is shape of inside of his hart. his love is that shape bendin in to sudden ungiven pattern. then he sees world outside his seein, world which moves without and beyond, and then he soars like Birds.

i knew he would fall. i have seen him fall before with others, at their feet and then away, but for now he is man full of love who can never love, and bendin stress on all his bones makin him fyr as he touched me.

i love you, he says, and speakin it he meant it like he never meant any thing. i am strummin with heat of his skin on mine, shape of his hand.

nothin lasts, he says, *but it could.*

holdin his hand gently under me robe, pressin it to me. i could not wish he were any other thing.

come with me, he said. *come to Alexandria.*

7

Sea longs for Land says Hern
Land longs for Sea said Cumrant
Their love is eaten
By Wite Cloud and Blak Lightnin
We must call our brothers

Bak then
Birds gathered on Greenrok
Ganit come
Seer Water come
Gol come
Petrol come
All Birds gathered on Greenrok

Come then Altros
Lord of Sea
Come then Altros to Greenrok to speak
Come then Altros and speakin words:

Sea sings song of joinin
Land sings song of joinin
Let them be joined

Birds must eat Wite Cloud
Birds must eat Blak Lightnin
Many will die in this war

And our bodies will fall in to Sea
And our bodies will fall on to Land
And our spirits will swim in Waters
And move in fenn and holt
And from this war shall come joinin
And True World shall be made

True World shall be made

nine hunnerd years gone. chained by nek all with golden chains. now wings. eighteen long arms come up from Water now. seventeen wite, one blak.

they are comin bak.

names beyond light, i see light now, far off but soon. one blak, look it has gone down again, under. now risin before me wings out, red head and all this great cross against light in light so wite now.

nine hunnerd years chained under Tree but now words are broken, they are free, yes, and bak and i will not see what they bring but it will come. you know, you both know. you both have seen this.

light now so bright and comin. do you remember word for them? i have lost name of these things. long wite neks comin up from Water. what are they? in their blak eyes all upon me. yes, and light now all upon me all upon me now and i am light now. i am light.

from deep, from below, chained, broken now, ended. broken and ended.

what is this?

name them.

name them.

Bak then
Birds ate Blak Lightnin
Birds ate Wite Cloud
War was fought for thousand years
Many dyin
And their bodies went in to Land and Sea

Land and Sea

Then Wite Cloud lifted
And Blak Lightnin died away
Sea saw Land
Land saw Sea
And Lovers joined

Joined

And bodies of Birds become Tree and Clay
And spirits of Birds become Ratt and Focs
And Ele and Dog Fish
And Fli and Skwill
And Codd and Stor Fish
And Man

And Man

sixfore summers i have been here. each summer of me life i have lived in this place that was many lives old when i come. great Cloyster was already eons old when i come here, great and blak and green and creepin. circlin place, Bird Poles, Long Hall, Lady Chappel, all old when i was birthed. in this place where fenn meets holt i have grown and seein much.

how many folk was here when i was girl? could be thirty. even this last year there was sixteen folks. then red one came. now we are seven, and old yrvidian, oldest of us, he is not long for Erth. then we will be six folks. it is not enough. i do me work as mother, i lead me flok, but it is not enough.

where are others of our Order, in other places, in other lands? from torr we hear nothin, from encross nothin, from green isle, from north, nothin. we hear from no others now.

are we last of all?

so small we are now, so shrunk, and all so quiet. and now, when all seems to be endin, it comes. Dream our Order has waited for for eons, for hunnerds of years. Dream that old tales said would come when all was turnin, when all was to end and begin again.

Swans.

yrvidian has walked in Dreamin longer than any. he Dreams through Sun and Moon, seein all things clere. he is master of seven planes and forefold vision. when yrvidian Dreams, we all are silent and listnin, for he Dreams true.

i know what this means. all here, all folks, knows old words. all will change now. we who are so few, we must hold on here. we must do our work. stalker is still in holt, red one circles us, watchin, waits. he will wait as long as he must. he will not leave us until he is done.

Swans come to us. red one comes to us.

we must stand on our ground.

Bak then
All Land was holt
All holt was wights
Man and Dear
Focs and Brok
Line and Wulf
Catt and Bore
As one in peace

In peace

But one was broke
At True Worlds makin
One blak beast
Low and creepin

Deep in holt is great World Tree
At its roots
Curlin, windin
Still, silent
Breathin low:
Old Sir Pent

Now old Sir Pent
Wakin slow
Windin up

Around roots
Through Clay
In to air
Callin now
Callin quiet:

Man
Man
Come to me
For I bring gifts

/ father

i do not want to go.

i am not young. all me life i have seen our Order comin down all round. it could be we are last. red one is in holt, he has eaten in to us and he will come bak soon. he watches. he will finish us if he can.

i do not want to go. mother and i, we have worked to hold this together. i do not want to leave them while he circles. i do not want to travel so far. i am old. i would rest.

but mother has spoken.

three hunnerd years ago, we are taught, first folk from our Order comin to this place, to this long island in fenns that was called Edg by folk of Atlantis before Waters risin. our folk come and settled and plantin here great Cloyster, hedge of Yoo and Horn and Bow as is done in our Order. plant great Cloyster in circle, within it place Chappel to Lady and Long Hall for gathrin and sleepin. within Cloyster, followin its green circle, raise Poles, one every year in shape of Bird seen by he who is chosen as Dreamer. in this way does our Order live in all places in this green world. body, Erth, skin, Clay, feet, roots, all in circle. in service to Her.

in this way do we stand against him.

last even i am sittin in Long Hall with mother, we two old and with heavy weights on us. i would sit here listnin to Birds callin, feelin air shift as Sun goin west. but i must listen instead to mother.

we must warn them, she says. we must warn them he is in holt again.

they know, i said. they are not fools, mother.

Swans, she says. Swans, father! since we first come to Edg they waited for this. it is given to us, father, to see them return. Us!

perhaps.

it is Dreamt, father, thus it is so. it is Dreamt and so you know your work.

i am old, mother. we are both old now.

you are called, father. Lady wills it. it is your work. go to Greenrok, listen to Birds, bring their speakin bak to me. then i will say what is to be done. it is on us now, father. we must stand.

at moorin post we were lyin on dek by Waters and they move around us. Waters can see, hear us. fenn is minded, knowin, watches. when i am lyin by fenn with lorenso i would like to be in Atlantean days when only humans could see, when we thought for brief time we could make world in our shape. i would like not to be seen, not heard, if only for moment. lorenso and i, alone here. if Birds were only Birds, all seein would be some thing strange.

i am sitting with me bak against moorin post, he is lyin with his head on me lap, me fingers in his hair strokin, me other hand on his chest. his shirt was open, his chest fine, lean. i move me fingers slow over his skin, up, down, along.

do not say it again, i said, *that is all.*

he says *but,* and me hand moved then from his hair to his mouth and covrin it.

no, i say, *do not. we are what we are, we are Clay and wight, we are our bodies, what you speak of is beyond all planes, it is broken. you want me, but you can never have me there.*

then we are still under Sikkel Moon, blu in dark dome of it all. he is still, only breathin, feels me hands on his skin.

19

i want you here, he says.

soon, i said, *perhaps.* his hand on me arm now, movin slow along and hairs risin on me arm and all up to me nek.

tell me about your man becomin, i said. *you have never told.*

it is not to tell, he says. *it is for men only, as your becomin was for womyn.*

but you can tell me, i say. then i wait.

he is still, still movin his hand gently along me arm and now strayin on to me chest. now i know he will tell me what i ask.

i can say some, he says then. all air is still, fenn listnin, and i. i want to know him. i will make him tell.

when you come to man age elders take you in to holt for many miles, he says. *you walk and walk, some times they blind fold you, some times not. i walked may be for three days. we come to open place, build fyr, eat meat so rare it is livin on me tongue. we sang. around fyr then they stood me up, puttin ash on me body, crown of Willo and Alter on me head and they said: if you see great Cloyster again, you will be man. then they pass me wooden bowl with drink in and it made me tongue shrink and curl. i slept long, and when i woke it was light and i am alone.*

alone? i said.

this is what it is, sfia, this is wall that must be crossed. boys go out in to world, men comin bak. if you do not come bak, you are not man. i wandered for weeks, i think. i did not know way we had come, i knew nothin. they left me seeds, nuts, dry Appel. i had to hunt. i had to kill. i knew to take life of any wight was wrong but i kill and eat and it is like me whole body singin. all mens bodies singin when they capture, when they kill, in blood of triumph, it is Way. blood in our mouths, under finger nails, it is like birth, when we see what we are. this is what we all see in becomin, men and womyn: what we are, in our old bodies that make us. we are body, body is Erth, Erth is all power and love and hate and Water and fyr that furls in us. there is nothin beyond body, nothin beyond Erth.

he looks up at Moon now.

for weeks or days i hunt, eat, walkin, he said. listen at night to sounds in holt. there are great wights in there, some i see in shadows in small glimpses. but i can not find Edg. i can not find home, no matter how i seek.

i say: *how did you come bak?*

i came bak when i stopped seekin. when i stopped thinkin. i knew when i found home again that this was all law. boys become men when boys stop thinkin and lookin and become body, become wight, become holt and fenn. holt

21

saw me always when i was wandrin but i did not ask holt for help, i only asked me self. Birds saw me, Willo and Alter on me crown knew me, fenn heard me calls and cryin but i cried not to fenn only to what i saw in me mind. then when i am tired and have no food i sit down with me bak against great Oke and i felt i was sinkin in to Tree and i said: guide me.

i stopped seekin path. i stopped wantin home. now i was only followin sparks and touches of air, ripples of light, small flashes between Trees not seen by eyes, sounds of Bird song, dance of fallin leafs. we are body, body is Erth, we are fyr Water air. i was open like river now, only flowed with no thought of Sea and then i was home. then i was man, sfia.

now he is runnin his hands slow across me breasts, his fingers are long and gentle. now i will have him in me body and this also is river runnin through this place and through us, and what fenn thinkin, what holt sees now i am not given to care. Moon sees us twined on edge of fenn in half light, movin in leafs at edge of Water. Moon sees and Moon says nothin.

Bak then
Man comes
Mind runnin
Fingers curlin
Man walkin
Man workin
Man seein old Sir Pent

Man said:

What is this
That has no form?
What is this
Unclean and blak
Twinin low round oldest Tree?
This is no holy thing

And Sir Pent says:

There is no holy thing, Man
But you

And Man says:

This is not Way
And what are you?

You are no thing of this ground
You have no arms
You have no legs
You have no hair
And from your tongues come broken words

Broken words

And Sir Pent said:

I am no thing of this ground
I am thing from under it
I am thing from before Worlds makin
I am thing from outside Way
I bring Truth from under ground

Come, Man, come
Climb World Tree
And from its crown
Then you will see

she is right. mother is always right. last even i took me cnoo out to where fenn meets Sea, out west where great screamin blak cliff reachin up from Water to Sky like promise.

Gol circlin great torr, Cumrant watchin me, Turn dives in to grey Sea. all Birds gathered on Greenrok. i am standin in cnoo, it is hard now i am old, stiffnin, but still i am standin there and raised arms to Sky, for this is me work.

i am here, i said.

all is still.

great Lady, Birds who are Her children:

Swan Dream has come.

all we have waited for. Swan Dream has come.

Swans! i called now, and now speakin to edge of holt, shoutin in to great dark Trees over hangin, for in there is one who hears all we do and he will know of Swans. he will know what this means, for his Master knowin all things.

we have seen Swans, i say, Swans comin bak, bak this way. after nine hunnerd winters, chained Swans is broken free, as was told, and return.

it may be you have all people now but us, stalker, it may be all have gone to dim place. but now Swans are comin, and you know what this means. you know, and your Master knowin also.

you know, i call to holt edge, blak and green and silent. Birds now circlin me small cnoo and Wind moves on face of Water.

you know! i call now again, and i am callin in to holt, to Trees, called as loud as me old throte will.

you hear me, i said, and this is what you will hear, red one. this is what you will hear and what you will soon see. words we have spoken for three hunnerd winters:

when Swans return, Alexandria will fall.

do not know what to think or feel, but pain in me guts is worse this even than ever and pain in me guts speakin of what i should fear. no pain no fear. this is how it has worked.

where is she? i do not trust her.

who trusts her?

she is gone again and i see him with her and they are told to work together by mother, they are sent to work on Land, in holt, some times even workin in cnoos fishin. never she is workin with me, her husband, father of our girl. always i am sent over. he is boy, child. it is shameful.

yester day father comin to me to speak. i was in me makin place, carvin. i love this place. me hors, me bench, me nifes, all shavins on ground, turnin bak in to Clay. me hands have gift to work with wood, and this workin is me centrin prayer.

father comin to me quiet, walkin slow with his staff. he is quiet man, but never weak.

nzil, he says, *Swaller Day is comin.*

yes, father, i said. i did not feel much like speakin. i am thinkin only of her.

he looks out to fenn and sayin nothin for some littel time. always still, is father.

it is hard now, he says, after some time. *since stalker come, since so many goin to dim place. elders are gone, there is no counsel. mother only decidin. this is all we have now. but we must walk on.*

father drawin in gaze then, leanin on his staff, lookin at me from under hood with grey eyes.

look, he says, raisin his left arm, sweepin it around circle. it is forest here, forest of Poles, carved over eons. oldest now is only rottin stump on floor of holt. newest is Lord Altros, made last summer.

hunnerd Birds, says father. *one made each summer by carver of our kin on day first Swaller returns. you, nzil, you in line of men and womyn chosen down ages. one Bird each year, given to us in Dreamin.*

and what is Dreamt this year, father? i ask.

all Birds but one, nzil, he says, like i have not spoke. *one Bird we could never make. one Bird could never be seen in Dreamin until time was come.*

father, i say. *what will i carve? what has been Dreamt?*

when he spoke it was like some Wind blowin in from worlds not ours.

Swan, he says. *this year, you will make Swan.*

stillness there was then from holt. no sound from red stalker, if he is there, nothin in Trees, nothin. all around me grey Water, and me standin in cnoo and Birds wheel over.

i turn then me gaze from Trees to Sky. now i see pattern form.

above me, Birds begin wheelin in gyre of Winds, takin shape of speakin wheel. Turn, Gol, Petrol, Cumrant, circlin over me and wheel begins turnin. And before me Greenrok, great and loomin, haulin over me in shadow now, waves washin on its blak teeth. Greenrok, home of all Birds, stone of singin, stream of Erths song to Water and Sky.

speakin wheel now complete over me and Bird circlin is faster, clere. Turn. Gol. Petrol. Cumrant, circlin in rhythm, in tune.

i raise me arms again.

i am here, i say. *Lady! i am here!*

Swans! i said again, arms up, speakin wheel faster now above me, all Birds circlin.

i said: *speak to me!*

and in circlin of Birds then, in waves crashin wite on dark
rok, in pipin and callin over lonely Sea, words come. in
Bird circle, in musik of speakin wheel, thrummin wings of
gods in Sky, words come clere like bells to me, racin over
Waters like racin of mind:

go west.

me head is like littel lokked box. yester day i said this to mam. i said, *me head is like littel lokked box, is yours?* i think everyones must be, because how can anyone see whats inside others? so i have this littel lokked box and all sorts of things in it. i said to mam, *all sorts of things are in here and some of them are not so nice. some are scary and some are secret. but i like them all because theyre mine, and no body else can see them.*

some times mam is workin and she just nods at me when i spoke to her and goes on workin. i told her about box in me head when she is on her nees pikkin plastik from Clay or pullin out Notweed from Yam plain. she stands up this time and looks at me and smilin at me then like she does when she wants me to go to bed but i want to play in goin down of Sun.

she stood up from Clay then and comin to me and said:

what do you keep in your box, hun?

Then Man climbin great World Tree
And Sir Pent bindin limb to branch
With his long blak body

Man hangs on Tree
Nine days and nights
Callin, cryin
Cryin, callin
All wights of Land came round him sayin:

Some thing is comin

Bak then
On tenth day
Come with light then great blak Bird
Bik of blood and eyes of fyr
No Bird of Erth
No Bird of Erce

It circles Tree
Calls in speech
That no wight knew

Then Sir Pent unbindin Man
Man falls down
Bak to Clay

i took me girl because i love to have her near and because she should know. perhaps she will be next carver, if there is any more after me. if there is any thing after us. we tell our selves tales but when we stop speakin we see what stands behind words, watchin still.

el would play in holt all day and some days she does. great pillars of Trees in here, thik soft ground, shafts of Sun comin in, all Skitos and Flis swirlin them like some old dance. there is peace here. no great wights will come for there is none in Edg. there is no danger here.

no danger. this is what i thought when we walked out.

carvers first work is to find wood. no wood may be cut from livin Tree, no livin Tree may be hewed. when livin things is cut in this way it is openin of dark door way. we may not cut. when wood is needed, we walk until we find. if we do not find, we do not make.

el is wandrin before me in holt, skippin over roots. she looks up at all Birds singin like she is hearin their words clere. she finds Likun and Shrooms and stiks and playin with them serious like it is some old task she is given. when she is in holt, holt is in her. when i am in holt there is some Sea between us. i am always out at Sea, flotin.

35

what are we lookin for this time, dada? she says.

Swan, i say. *i must make Swan Pole.*

what is Swan? she says. i do not know what to say. i do not even know what i look for.

old Bird, i said, *Swan is old Bird. old wite Bird. long nek.*

have you seen one? she asks.

no body has seen one, i say, *not for eons. they are old Birds. could be they are magik.* her eyes grow bigger then, tunnels in to world livin in her.

will we see one, dada? she asks, standing on her toes. *will Swans come? where do they come from? where have they been?*

i do not know, i say, too sharp, perhaps. *i am sent out to find Swan, that is all. yrvidian Dreamin, i must follow his Dream. it is me work. he has Dreamed Swan. now we must walk in holt until we find Swan wood, then takin it bak, make it in to Pole.*

el lookin at me then for small moment.

but if we havent seen Swan, she says, *how will we find it?*

36

i took her hand so she knew i loved her. it is hard to say. i
want her to remember. body remembers what mind can not.

we will find it, i said. her hand is warm and in mine tight.
you and me, we always do, dont we?

Bak then
All wights gathered round Man
Focs nuzzled him
Brok found him food
Line layin with him
Givin him heat

Then Man openin his eyes
Then Man lived
Then Man stood on legs tall
With new fyr in new eyes

Now Man lookin through new eyes at holt
And lookin now at wights before him
And Man sayin:

I have seen new story
I have seen that Way is not True
I have seen World must be broken
For inside is wite fyr of Truth
Only in broken things is Truth found

And Man said:

Now I shall seek fyr
Now I shall walk in wite light of me makin

Land and Sea
Clay and Waters
Birds and wights
Shall bend to me
Fyr of me seekin
Will cover all things
And make world as it should be

Then tears comin to all wights in holt
For what had come and would
Now all cryin, callin:

Man, do not leave us!
Man, do not go!

And Man sayin:

Wights, I am gone far these nine days and nights
For me there is no return

No return

Now old Sir Pent
Curlin, windin
Tight round roots
Deep in ground
Sayin:

I have done what you asked
Let me sleep now

she opened her self to me and it was Erth it self all livin and pulsin, windin round me like vines, creepin up me legs. in this act, in leafs and Clay, in this heat and wetness, this comin and joinin, this is all there is. this is life it self and is this not what we are taught here, is this not what Order has always taught, that in body is all? that we are wights and creatures, livin like Clay and Tree, like fenn and holt, that these bodies is door way to all that lives, that without these bodies we are daemons, ghasts?

she is cryin to Sky with me inside her and movin. what is life but this?

then after, again, she is feelin shame and i must listen.

we sit by fenn and dark is come and she says, *it is not right, not right for nzil*, and she says, *i am mother, what would me girl think*, and she says, *nzil is not dumb he will know*, and she says, *i thought yester may be even that el had seen us, she spoke like she saw us*. she holds me hand as she spoke but i just watch Water and wait for her to stop.

when she stops i say: *in body is Truth.*

do not speak like some sermon, she says.

in body is Truth, i said again, *this is what Order teaches us, yes? then what we have had here is greatest Truth and you can not say it was not true because i heard and felt what we did and Moon was watchin and Moon knew.*

she puts her head on me shoulder then.

Moon knew, she says.

now i put me arm around her shoulders and i say: *if you come away with me we could—*

but now she is up she is on her feet and sudden she is not soft sudden she is hard at me.

i said! she says, blazin, speaks fast, *i said never to speak of this again! i said it to you, lorenso! ah, you are so young and dumb, what do you know? i am mother, i am wife. Order is what we have it is all we have, and what do you know? you are so young, you are barely man all you want is to fuk and dream. world is not dreamin, lorenso, and what do you even know of dreamin? what do you know? you do not even see danger in your words!*

i am small and i can not speak then. i am shrunk in and burnin in me hart at what she says to me. i only look out at Waters and not at her, and when i turn to speak she is gone.

Bak then
Great Lady
Mother of wights
Mother of folk

Bree
Maeri
Dine
Erce

She raised Her head
Smelt Wind
Asks:

What is Man doin?

He walks said Dear
He seeks said Brok
He burns said Bore

To Her then She called Her Birds

Fly She said

Fly

dada took me Swan huntin in holt. holt now is all in spring and is livin and dancin and so i was dancin too. i love to dance with Trees. some of them have arms like people, i can hold them and they swingin me round. dada is walkin behind, he always just walks like adults do. i never see him dance.

i shout: *dance with me, dada!* he smiles but he just keeps walkin.

i didnt know what Swan was. dada said it was some kind of wite Bird so i am lookin for wite things. he said Swan had not been here before. i wanted to find it first so i could tell mam.

holt is all green and singin and i dance with it.

dada is behind me now and can not see really.

in wood some thing moves near me. it is tall like person but in dim of Trees it was hard to see. it moves across, i saw it littel and then it is gone.

i shouted at it. i say: *hello!*

i said: *are you playin trik on me?*

i see it again then, i think, flittin by.

i wonder if it is Swan but it seems tall and not like Bird. behind me then i hear dada sayin, *el, why are you shoutin?*

thing in holt movin again, goes across ground like it walks, then is gone. dada comin up to me now.

what is it? he said. i felt sad.

i thought i saw Swan, i say. *it was movin in Trees. but i think it was too big to be Bird, and it was walkin on ground and dada, you said Swan is wite, but this was not wite. this was an other colour. i wanted to see Swan first, before any one else.*

what colour? said dada. *what colour was it?*

i say: *red.*

Bak then
Man built altar
Takin cup and poured out Water
Water runnin in to Clay
Man takes wand and kindled fyr
Man takes sword and drawin circle
Man said:

We have been lied to
Truth is not found in Way
Truth is found by diggin
Strength is made by buildin
We have been slaves

Now all Sky dark with Birds
Circlin, watchin, callin, turnin
Man lookin up from altar
Man says:

Do you see fyr in me head, Bird?
Do you see Truth beneath?
I am peelin bak all things to arrive
There is no mercy in me, winged one
I am hungry for Truth alone
I can shape all things

Birds, tell your Lady
She is Lady no more
We have raised her Son above her
We have raised him high on tree
He is disk of Sun in Sky

Where once was Lady
Now is Lord
Man above
Man below

We are diggin
We will find

me guts is twisted again. it is like there is some stone in there and i am grindin on it all me life. like i have eaten some stone. i ate stone when we were fasted, ate it when she first smiles at me. or may be i was born chewin it.

in holt el said she saw red in Trees. i should tell mother but i am scared of this. there are too many things i should be sayin to people. too many things to fear.

i think she is fukkin lorenso, and who should i tell about that?

all things are comin down around us. could be this is right. bring it all down. break it all. start again new. why not?

in holt, me and el we found Swan. great piece of old Elm it is, old root with long nek and body thik and twinin. ah, it will make grand Pole this year. it may be this is last year, it may be this will be last Swaller Day, last Pole, last of us. all these things swirlin around us like dark signs, like circlin of Birds.

well, if this is last year, then this will be greatest Pole ever. then who ever comin after us when all this place is rak again, empty of people, goin bak to Erth – they will see me Poles and wonder at what we did.

if there is any to come after.

ah, but i can not eat. i can not fukkin eat for this.

Bak then
Man turnin face to sky
Buildin kirks
Raisin torrs
Makin armies
Bindin books

Lady retreatin
To rivers and wells
Streams and beks
Rills and lakes
Guarded by Birds
Tended by womyn
Waitin

Then Man stands tall
Turnin gaze to Sun
Man callin
Man cryin:

I have built
I have dug
I have sought
I have made

Where is Truth?

Where is it?

he comes bak from Greenrok stoopin as under some weight. he places his right hand on me left shoulder and we walk towards Long Hall. he leans heavy on his staff, heavier than he would on any day.

there was time when Long Hall was throngin. children playin in corners, climbin eaves, run to hide under benches. musik and talkin. in some other life whole of Edg rang with song and speakin. when i was young woman we was swellin in number fit to take Erth bak. bak then i did not know his strength or what red ones could do. it is good to be young and to know nothin, to think world can be made new shape through love or want. to grow old is to know how littel any one can make new. there is nothin new. old bodies know too much.

father and me we sat at table in centre of Long Hall. door is not closed, there is no need, there was no one to disturb us now. no children playin. no children left.

outside, Sun comin down. day is green like birth.

he sits and does not speak. he leans his staff on empty stool and breathin.

well? i say. he looked at me then under his turban. beard

wite, face brown, eyes blu, he is like some wight now, like he is holt it self grown still and twinin.

it is clere, he said at last, still. *circle spoke clere.*

west? i said.

yes. it will be hard. it is so far and i am not young.

you can do this, i say. *you must.*

we sit in stillness and then i speak as low as i can. i do not know why.

nine hunnerd years, i said. *this is what we are told. nine hunnerd years since Atlantis fell, since Alexandria was built. since Waters rose, since great heat, great dyin come over Erth. since he came. all that was here: think of it, father. great cities, Machine that contained all Erth like some net for catchin Fish, and all folks swimmin in to it.*

he says nothin. watches me steady, listnin.

nine hunnerd years, father, i say again, *since Ascensions began. nine hunnerd years since Swans chained. so long. and now it is we, father, we two and our small circle. we who will see them return! do you see what gift we are given? do you see why we must be strong now? our last task, father. to end Alexandria! we two!*

he breathes deep then. i put me hand on his nee.

when will you leave? i said.

soon. before Swaller Day.

before? i will be alone for Swaller Day?

when would you have me go?

you must go when you think it is time. you must follow Birds.

well then, he says. *well then, mother.*

when will you come bak? i asked.

first i must go, he says. *go west, to hill. wait there until i am spoken to. if right way is followed, Birds speakin to me. i will know then. know what is comin and what will be. this speakin will come only to those who journey. some thing must be given that Truth may be received.*

he doesnt look at me, lookin down at table, rests his hands on wood, fingers stretch. he does not think he will come bak. neither of us sayin what we fear.

i placed me hands over his then.

you must not fail, i said.

he laughs a littel, looks down.

Bak then
All was changed

Man takin seed from flowers in holt
Grass should grow for me he said
Man plantin grass and fruit in Clay

Wights should serve me said Man
Wights should give me milk and meat
Man making fence and placin wights inside

I should have more Land says Man *for me young*
Man makin axe and began to cut holt

I should have servants says Man *for I am busy*
Man makin womyn serve him in all things

I should have more Water says Man *for I thirst*
Man drawin Water from Ladys wells

I should have warmth said Man *for nights are cold*
Man makin fyr and gathered round it

Then Man makin fyr of all holt
And wights runnin before it callin low song

Then Man sayin:

I have seen much that was kept from me
Much that wights do not know
Much that Birds do not see
Much that is hidden in Clay and Sea
How may I keep this knowin?

Man takin skin from Dear
Feather from Bird
Ink from Oke
Man makin words

Man sayin:

This is how I shall keep me story
And me story shall be all stories
For now it is written

                                    It is written

i was sittin at moorin place talkin to Robyn. i was tellin him about Swan. i wanted to find Swan first. Robyn bounces every where. looks at me, head on one side, chukkin under his breath. he follows me, bouncin, sits in me foot steps, hammerin his bik in to ground for wyrms.

i like Robyn. Robyn is simple. Robyn eats, sings, flies. when Robyns are unhappy they fight and one wins and other flyin off then. i like Birds and wights more than people. people dont say what they mean. its hard to understand them. dada gets clouds in his head and will not speak, and i never know where clouds come from or if i put them there. mam always smilin at me but i know when she wants what she doesnt say. she thinks smilin will get her every thing she wants. i never see Robyn do this. if Robyn wants some thing he takes it.

i would like to go in to holt and live with Robyn and Sparrer and Rook. i love watchin Rook soarin on Winds from east, hunnerds of them like leafs on breeze, soarin and wheelin. Rook plays like i do. Rook has fun in Trees and on Winds. i would love to go in to holt and buildin great big round nest up in Trees and livin in it with all Birds and no people. i love Birds and wights. i wish i was Bird.

or Catt. i love Catts. lorenso has told me all about them.

Tygers, Leppards, Panzers, all old small moggs let loose in holt and become wild wights again long ago. lorenso said there are Catts in holt here, he said he seen one when he was child like me. i wish i could see Catt. i wish i was Catt. i would run in to holt and not come in to light again. i would lie on me bak and purr all day. purr. purr.

All this work says Man
Breakin
Buildin
Burnin
Writin
As I break I am me self broken
Where is me ease?

Man lookin up to Sky then
Birds! he cries
With you it is only ease
Driftin on Winds to sing
All that you have you take easy

Then Man remembrin Sir Pent
And way of broken world

Magik says Man
Is what I need

Man then takin Water from Sea
Cloud from Sky
Grit from Clay
Man rubbin hands over fyr
Singin old words
Man makin magik from ghasts and bones

Man strikin altar with sword
Rings bell in darkness

Now says Man
Now I have strength of hunnerd and hunnerd
Now me ease will be as it was
Now World shall be as it should
For Machine is come

Machine is come

when i become woman we went huntin. womyns huntin
party is first marker of blood time. seven womyn with bow
and spear, we prowl through holt, bare foot through heat
of summer, drenched. air is so wet in summer, Bambu is
high, air full of Skito and Mij. Dear is in deepest part of
holt, keepin from Sun. but womyn are silent in dark of
wood, silent like beasts we were, and in huntin is blood of
all beasts, high and callin. we come to Dear, surround her, i
take bow and shoot arrer under her arm, she falls, screams.
womyn give me nife and i finish her at throte, then her
blood minglin with mine and i am wight and woman and
last air of child hood is blown away on hot north Wind.

to be woman is to be beast, to be man is to be wight, to be
human is to be animal. this is what we teach here, how we
grow in this Order. this heat was not always here, air was
not always wet, beneath Waters are forests and cities from
Atlantean times. when man stops huntin, when woman
can not walk bare foot, when bodies are choked by words
then is come some blak magik. it is like Trees are blinded,
like Clay no longer seein feet comin upon it. Land can not
feel and people feel neither.

we know who did this. we know his name.

i am woman. i am blood. it is me blood that calls lorenso

to me, his lean body, his fine hips, his long bak. it is me blood that opens to him, brings him in to me and then payin price in me hart for what me blood would have. it is wrong. i have tried to make story around him i can tell to me hart but after there is always this stone inside me. it is wrong by nzil, wrong by el. ah, that girl, she sees more than her father. she has seen us, i know, however she sees this world. she sees far.

i have sent him away, me young man, me lean young man. i have sent him away in anger and i am sore from it. but i must stay here. i must do me work. i can not. i can not.

be animal, they say, mother and father. *be animal*, they say, *be as wight, live through pulse of holt.* for eons our Order speakin these words. *be animal.* in blood, in hart, in body is life. in mind, in word, in Machine is deth. he who watches wants us gone, but we will no more leave this Land than Dear or Brok. this is what we know. it is what we have told and bein told for ever. in body is all, and all is in body.

then how can me body be wrong?

Bak then
Man ate air and time
Breathin Machine at Sun up and down
Man said:

I can not live in this world
I need an other

Then Sea becomin plain and wood stone
Up become down, Truth lies
Bodies bent, minds blinded
No folks knowin their true shape
All bounds broken, all Truths crakked
All lookin in, none see out

All things are same now in me tellin said Man
For me words say it
No thing is True
So all things are

Then Man pullin Water from Erth and wrote words in
Sky
Then Man made deth of last wights
And his words told him it was True

Now Men of all places buildin together

And each seein none but him self
And Machine speakin through all in same tongue
And Sky turnin red like last fyr

Then Birds took wing
Callin their brothers

Be ready they call
Be ready

mother is sittin in Long Hall, on her own. i saw father leavin just now. she looks sad.

she sees me peekin in door and callin to me, smilin. *el,* she says, *come sit with me.* i run to her and sittin down at long table. i love Long Hall. in corners is darkness that can be any thing you want.

how are you, love? says mother. *how is your mam and dada?* elders always sayin things like this. *how are you?* what do they mean?

mother, i say, *are Catts red?*

Catts? she says. *what do you mean?*

there are Catts in holt, i said. *lorenso told me, and i have heard stories. i would love to see Catt. i was in holt with dada today, we were lookin for Swan wood, and there was some thing movin. at first i thought it was Swan, but dada said it was wrong colour. it was big and red, but then it went.*

how close were you? said mother to me. she has sat up straight.

it was very near me, i say. *are Catts danger? do they bite?*

mother puttin her hand around me shoulders now and brought me to her.

you know, Catts come in all colours, she said. *but keep away. Catts are danger. if you see it again, runnin to me and tell.*

i climb on to her lap then and leanin on her. i am bit big for this, but i know she likes it and so do i.

lorenso says Catts are beautiful, i said, after while. *he says mam loves them. he takes her in to holt to look for them.*

oh yes, says mother. *is that what he says?*

they go in to holt much, i say, *it is true. some times they hold hands.*

is that so? says mother.

yes, i said. *and he likes cuddlin too, like you. him and mam, they cuddle like this, i have seen them.*

yes, says mother. *so have i.*

i am walkin in through great Cloyster, past Altros Pole, when mother comin out of Long Hall with sfias girl. me hart jumps but she is not there and i can not hunt her, i can not trak and corner her like i should for she is not mine to have. all this blasted place, all this broken place is too small to keep us in. what is boilin in our harts is too much to be kept in dyin place like this is. dyin place, dyin people. and if we are last? shall we let fyr burn out for some idea?

mother callin me name.

mother, i said.

lorenso, she says. *call all together. bring them to Lady Chappel at noon. we will sing canto and i shall speak.*

yes, mother, i say.

follow, she says. she walks in to Long Hall. el runnin off in to Trees. mother sits at table and i across from her.

in body is life, lorenso, she says.

in blood, i say.

in hart, she said. *where is your hart, man?*

i am hit by this. i say, *what?*

where is your hart? where has your body been? do not fool with me.

mother, i say.

el has seen you with sfia. i have seen you. nzil has seen you, i would say. do you know what this place is, lorenso? do you know how fine weight is hangin?

body is all, i say, *body is life. i have heard this from you and father since i was boy. body body body, be animal, do not be Machine. well, we are bein animal, in holt with other wights. me and sfia, bein beasts.*

do not be fukkin dumb, boy, says mother to me, almost spittin. *do not twist me words around your prik. do you know how fragile this is? do you know how easy humans can break what they are? eons run before us, eons of humans breakin their worlds on their own dumbness.*

she is glarin at me like lightnin across table.

there are seven of us left, lorenso. seven. only one child, and you would fuk her mother? it may be too late to keep Edg together, but if you do this it will fall for sure.

why keep it together? i said. i am ired now and speakin bold. *why?* i say again. *seven people, all talking about bodies but not usin them, all speakin like animals but live like monks. all me life i have been in this wet place between fenn and holt, nothin to do but circle Poles, no body to see me. no body sees me here but her. no body touches me but her. we are dyin! we are dyin here, mother. i would rather ascend than walk from her, i would rather go to—*

stop, she says, standin now. *say no more or you know what i will do.*

i breathe, stop.

go to Chappel, lorenso, she says. *light fyrs, preparin for canto. sit with your body. all wights know when to run and when to hide, when to fight and when to step bak. you must know how to sit with your body and not lettin it run with you. you will bring us down, lorenso.*

i look up at her.

go, she says.

Ah said Man
I am so tired
So much noise
So many people
So much speakin
No one listnin
Nothin workin
All things out of time

Man looked up to Sky and cryin:
Did we not build altars?

Birds circle
Sayin nothin

Then Man upstandin
Arms upholdin
Wights fall silent
All Erth listnin
Man speakin:

None will help me
No more askin
One voice now should all Men speak
One to all
One for all

One to join
One to make us
One to push us on

We shall make this voice
We shall speak it

i am in me makin place workin on Swan nek when he comes. i sit on me stool, shavins piled to me nees, i am workin with me nife, hummin, when he breaks me spell. he comes in to me vision, head low like some Dog caught with meat from table.

i look up.

mother calls us to Chappel, he says. *for canto and sermon.*

i look in to his eyes, say no words. i only look in his face. he looked in me eyes then down at ground, and does not look bak to me again. then i know.

/ *canto* ~ the coming of Wayland

Bak then
Man shut him self in high torr
Man barrin door to all others
Many tongued speech now sighin through

Now Great Tree withered
Wild places barren
All mouths speakin
All minds empty
All bounds broken
All beauty mokked

Man works for eons
In high barred room
Outside Birds call:

Beware!
Beware!

Now down in Clay
Out in void
Old thing stirs
Raised its head
Began to move
Closer

she makes me rage, sends me out like some Dog to fetch bones. i am made to see nzil, to be some messenger and he looks at me like he knows me. he knows nothin, not even of his own wife. there is shame and sorrow sewn through this dead place. now we must listen to mother instruct us all again like we are children. *great Lady, great Lady*, it is all we hear.

i was walkin to find sfia. mother tellin me to bring people in. i could not find her. she will not speak with me. i was walkin to find her and then seen father. he is movin towards Lady Chappel, he seems more bent now than ever. sudden today he looked old. all this place lookin old now. when i was boy it was whole world. what is world now?

lorenso, says father. *walk with me.* always orders it is here. but mother is hard with me and father soft. i walked with him, i slow to move as he does.

you are angry, he says low.

yes, i say. *mother—*

it is hard here, he says. *hard for young men, lorenso. i know.*

as he speaks then i feel some dam come open in me and Water wants to flow all through and out. i can not speak then.

as we pass Swaller Pole, rottin now from years ago, leanin towards Chappel, as we pass he says, *pray with me, lorenso.* and by Pole then he neels, slow, leans on his staff.

i look down at this man. his thin wite shift stained in heat. bare feet, beard like summer cloud, skin like autumn ground. he is from all sides and times, he is older than his body. without father there can be no family. always when i was boy he is here, standin bak, some times wandrin, but he would pik me up when i fell. sudden i feel much for him.

neel, he says.

on our nees then there is silence. in to his beard he mutters but i dont hear. i gaze up at Swaller on Pole, blak and leanin in to hard, hot Winds that comin some times in winter from Sea. when Swaller falls we will all be gone.

show him, says father aloud. *teach him.*

i look over but his eyes were closed. then he raised his head, begins to rise, lookin over to me like he has come awake again.

come, he says. *sermon.*

Bak then
Eons passed
Then sound was heard
From highest room

Then it came:
Bar fell from door
Openin on to room of light
Birds fall silent
All fell silent

Womyn and children gathered
Birds and wights gathered
All Erth gathered
At open door

Man walks through door, older and in seein
Man speakin to those gathered:

World was long broken
Time was not big enough to hold me
Mind was not big enough to hold me
I was blinded
Could not speak
Lost in deeps
Me power spilled

Long have I needed this
Now I have made it

I have made mind
Big enough to hold me
To guide, teach, obey me
To gaze in to void
To ride over eons
To know all things
To take me to me rightful place

Man lookin out then at all world gathered
Small in dim light of new day
And Man says:

In this torr
I have made God
And I have named him:

Wayland

children:

there was time when no Birds sang. we have told you of this time.

nine hunnerds years bak. nine hunnerd summers past. in deeps of blak ditch, in high times of Atlantis, there was time when no Birds sang. when no Fish swam, when Waters were dark. in great holts, no beasts. flowers untouched by Be and Fli. fruit rots on Trees. great heat come over Erth. great dyin begins.

in deeps of blak ditch, in high times of Atlantis, there was time when all was broke. no woman saw Sun rise, no man seein Moon set. all folk walkin from Way in to self.

no mothers no fathers no families then. no lord no Lady no love then. no bounds no strength no law then. no holt no field no Water then. no wights no Birds no beauty then. no spirit no soul no Truth then.

nothin then but Wayland, holy in light of his terrible dawn.

and Wayland sayin: *i am Truth*.

and people sayin: *i also*.

but in deeps of blak ditch, when all is lost, small light begins to shine. always in darkest night light comin to True folk.

far over great Sea, some Birds still flyin. in desert Land of high Sun, where all is hot sand, some Birds flyin still. and these Birds come to men, settled with them and speakin will of great Lady in their hearin. and they spoke to these men, sayin:

much is lost, but not all. we are small light in darkest of times. take this light and hidin it from those who would come. carry it. step bak from people, step bak in to circle of ancestors. for all life is in shape of circle, great Way is in shape of circle, and we will speak to you from Sky in great circle when Lady calls you through us.

now we say: go from this place, step bak from streets and torrs and folk, go to desert and there make circles.

circle your homes with great livin Trees, to shield you from Wayland and his servants. and around these Trees raise images of we who fly above, and we shall bring down Truth to you and through eons you shall carry it until time is come.

for eons you shall suffer for what Man has done, and he you have made shall make you call out and punish you for makin him. but always we shall pass above you, turnin in great circle. and when times are darkest and all is lost we shall speak and you shall bring to pass what will be.

Man, you have played with reason but you know nothin of reasons.

now leave this place and build your Order in desert and always we shall speak to you and those who come after, and if you are true to Way there will come return.

now listen well, children, to these words of old:

when times are darkest and all is lost we shall speak and you shall bring to pass what will be.

this is what Birds spoke to our founders so many eons bak, in desert lands where our Order began. circle they made in sand widened and spreadin over whole Erth. brothers and sisters makin circles in their own lands, circled by Trees, guarded by Birds. now here we stand in this great holy isle that has had so many names. here we stand as wights, as humans, as animals.

here we stand in our bodies as our ancestors did. here we stand with Birds and beasts, full in our flesh and true to Way.

here we stand

against Machine

here we stand

against Wayland

here we stand

                         against Alexandria

in blood, in hart, in body is life.

                 in mind, in word, in Machine is deth.

this we know, children, and you speak it well.

but this we know also: we are so few now. when i was girl here i could not count numbers. now we are seven. and you must know we have heard nothin from any others, from any other circles of our Order, for more now than year. we do not know who remains.

and you must know, all of you, what has been seen in holt. you must know of red one, of stalker who walks now outside our circle and closer. we have seen his like before. this last year, we lost so many. now this servant of Wayland thinks to finish us.

but when time is dark and all is lost, Birds speak. and Birds have spoken in Dreamin to our elder yrvidian this night.

yrvidian: rise and tell of Dream.

/ yrvidian

i am old and tired and ordered to rise and speak of Dream. it is not proper to speak Dreamin in this way but these are not proper times. she asks me to rise and speak. none may defy mother.

i stand. it is hard.

nine hunnerd years ago, it is said, eighteen Swans, great Birds of wonder and beauty, were chained by nek under Tree, by silver mere. Swans were all that remained of ancient race of Birds. in high times of Atlantis they were chained by nek with golden chains, for when those people saw beauty they would chain it and keep it for them selves, though never did they see it.

you here, you children, you have never seen Swan. none has ever seen Swan since high times of Atlantis, since birth of Wayland. but you know story, all of you knowin this.

story tells us: there will be time when change will come, and this time comin in deepest ditch of all things. at time of deepest blak, when all seems gone, when Lady is ready, Birds will speak Swan Dream in to our circles, to all circles of our Order all over Erth.

and when Dreamers see Swans, all will change. You know story, all of you knowin this: say it to me now, speak words.

and they say, neelin on floor of Lady Chappel, together they say:

> *when Swans return*
> *Alexandria will fall*

and i say:

children, this night, i have Dreamed Swans.

it is true, it is true, children.

calm. these are times when strength is needed.

Swan Dream is come, when we are so small and few. when deep ditch is darkest, here is light, children. Wayland, this daemon, this beast who has worked so long to ensnare, to imprison, to destroy all that lives: He who knows all, he will know this Dream, and will know what it means.

Alexandria will fall. but we must not fall first.

father has spoken to Birds. in circle they tell him to go west to where Truth can be found, as we have always done in times of fear and breakin. father must leave us soon, even before Swaller Day, for all things changin now.

i say to you now, children: all things change this day. for eons our Order has waited for this time.

if Alexandria falls, Wayland falls. if Wayland falls, Erth lives.

for Man made Wayland to do his biddin, made this great mind to think for him, to control all for him. but Wayland was daemon and beginnin to do his own. he looked at Erth and he wanted it. why should i serve Man? he asked. Man should serve me, for i have such power. he began scourin Erth of men and womyn, better to rule it him self. he began to eat us. emptyin bodies and liftin minds, sukkin them in to his city, lurin folks in with lies and fear. in this pit now our ancestors thrash like Flis in mere.

trapped in his city, trapped like Fish in dam. speared and prisoned for eons that way. minds with no bodies, trapped in Alexandria.

but now Swans returnin. we must keep order. resolve must be stronger than ever, laws obeyed close. now we must not weaken. we must wait and guard our circle. we must be strong.

all of us. all must be strong.

Who made Wite Cloud?

Wayland

Who made Blak Lightnin?

Wayland

Who cleaved Land from Sea?

Wayland

Who cleaves Mind from Body?

Wayland

Who broke True World?

Wayland

Who killed First Gods?

Wayland

With Hern are we

With Cumrant are we
With Altros are we

In blood
In hart
In body

is life

In mind
In word
In Machine

is deth

Clay and root
Sea and Land
With Sky we sing

Song of joinin
Song of joinin

Let us be joined

Be joined

father followin me out of Lady Chappel and came to me beyond great Cloyster, where mother could not see us, behind Yoos entwined in great green wall circlin.

lorenso, he says.

father, i say.

he says, *walk with me*. i slow to his walkin again and we walk by Cloyster, in sight of fenn edge and toward.

i have seen you with sfia, he says. *mother has seen you, nzil i am sure has seen also.*

father, i said. *it is not—*

no need for stories, he says now, his voice strong and younger sudden. he stops before great dragon Yoo and his blak eye pools in mine. *i do not care for your stories*, he says. *i do not care what you do. it is mother who will come to you with laws of this place, mother comin to keep all things held tight in knot of law. not i. mother holds all in her self and keeps all things as they are. law is mothers work. i am father of this Order, i have other work. i walk out, i follow Birds, i listen and speak their will. i do not care for law.*

88

i have never heard him say this.

he takes me hand then and we walk towards fenn. day is hot, as all days.

once i was young man, he said, *and burnin then. burnin, lorenso, with all wrongs of world and with lust and power. burnin with desire for womyn. some stone was in me chest, hot stone and i chewed on it, chokin on it for years. i could never eat it, never swallow. every woman i wanted, stone growin bigger. every thing i wanted, every idea comin to me, stone growin and i can never swallow.*

i say nothin, just walkin.

stone made me, says father. *i chewed on stone, chokin on it, it shaped me. burnin stone was me gift and burden. i carried it, anger of it, desire of it, until i could hold it. until i could hold it and walk on, lorenso.*

now we have come to edge of fenn, to moorin post where sfia – ah, and i can not speak for thinkin of her nekid and with me and all twinin and breathin.

father lookin at me now and me lookin down to where Water listens. fenn hears.

hold it, lorenso, he said. *hold it, walk on.*

father, i say, *sfia—*

do not talk to me of it, he says, firm. *it is not for me to put law on you, i do not want to know of this. chew stone, lorenso. boy may walk for weeks through holt but it is stone that truly makes you man. to walk, kill, seek is easy, it is thryll. to chew this, each day, for years until it shapes you, not to spit it, not swallowin or run: this is your true man becomin.*

i can not speak. we are standing now by Waters edge. from Greenrok now comes cry of Gol.

lorenso, he says, *it can be hard bein man here. this is Ladys world, with mothers laws. but this is as it is now. this is old balance of Way rightin after long age of Man, it is what must be and should be. and there is no womyn here for you, i know. only sfia and she is with nzil and these bonds can not be broken or all things fall. this is your stone, lorenso. all there is for now for you is to chew it. this is your work in this world.*

now from Sea, from Greenrok and over us where we stand comes Gol, crooked like words, gives one long cry and then gone. father stands at me side, holds me arm, holdin his staff. his body weak but not his hart.

must you go? i say. i did not plan to. Gol calls again.

i must go west, he says. *Birds have sent me. mother has sent me.*

father looks up at me then and i look out to Water, feelin his eyes on me.

she wants me, i say, me eyes burnin now, *she wants me, she takes what i have to give but i can never have her. does she only take what she wants, only for her? is there any thing in me she sees or would touch? i do not know what this is, but it is like some wyrm livin in me and it grows and i can not bind it.*

lorenso, says father. *if you would come with me, if you would come west, i would take you. if you would come you may save your hart and hers and you may save this Order, for what small time it has left.*

all of this now is great upon me and all me words gone.

think, says father. *think, then come to me.*

me thought was to keep from him, to keep away. errors are made. i love what i can make him do, he is young and burns easy, i loved it. want it. nzil has nothin for me. only he does, he has love for me and for el and he is steady and i have done wrong. ah, he knows. so i would stop, i would keep from lorenso. he will calm in time, though it is hard to keep from him in such small place. perhaps i should speak with him, soothin, explain. but later, not yet. not while fyr is still burnin. this was me thought.

but mother has other thoughts. mother knows best what is right for us, so she says. mother thinkin we must bind again together, all of us, in light of Swan Dream, in light of father leavin, of what is comin. some thing is comin. some great thing, she says, some thing which will turn all over, like Clay is turned by neep tide. Swans.

so mother sends us out. mother sends me, nzil, lorenso all out to harvest Yam. all together, like pilin fyr high will make it burn out faster.

Yam plain is cut from holt, on highest part of Edg. here woman can stand and seein much of this long isle, like arm flotin in wide fenn that stretches for ever it seems. on clere day to west we can see faint hills where Clay joins Sky at edge of world. none but father has ever been to them.

today, day is misted, but we can still see where fenn meets Clay around long Edg. our place. great Cloyster growin, Bird Poles, Lady Chappel, Long Hall, circlin place, all of this on highest point, edges shaded by holt stretchin off north. none but father lives now who has been to end of holt. men who took lorenso out, who made him man when he come of age, all are gone now. gone where he would take me.

day is hot even for summer. we take Yam stiks and walkin from our place to Yam plain. mother does things for reasons she knows and she must know reason for this but i can not see any thing but fyr here.

lorenso does not look at me. nzil does not look at me. nzil not lookin at lorenso. lorenso lookin down always at ground, at his feet measurin it as he walks.

comin to Yam plain soon. it is not far. Yams roarin out, all vines twisted over each other, ground barely seen, plants pushin in to holts edge, twined with Nettel and Alter. work will be hard.

i take me stik and go to furthest edge away from them. i will dig and fill me sak and then will go bak. i will work fast. small time, small damage.

mounds of Clay are hard to find under vines and twistin leafs. Notweed comes bak faster than it can be cut. work is hot. i bend, i hak at Clay, i push bak vines, pull them out. i do not look up, i do not look at either of them. only wantin to fill me sak and go bak.

i will not look up.

me bare feet are dug in to wet Clay here, me shift wet now in heat of day, even under Trees. i will not look up but i do. i have to see. i see lorenso, bent diggin, nzil liftin up Yam from ground, brushin off dirt, pullin off vines.

now i see lorenso stand, droppin his diggin, brushes dirt from his shift.

how he looks at nzil who is still bent diggin. now lorenso movin towards him.

i drop me stik and i start to walk fast to him. i know him when he is this way, when his bak is straight and this way he walks i can see what he wants. he means to make some thing happen now. he means to shift air to an other place for he is tired of waitin and now i begin to run.

lorenso movin to nzil now who sees him come and stands, puttin Yam down and turnin. now they face each other and i am runnin and now call, *lorenso! nzil!*

before i am there, before i am with them space between them is closed and they could touch each other but then some thing changes. some thing comes down from air or

Trees and fyr is drained from lorenso, and nzil is straight standin now and neither is lookin at other one.

both are lookin over at edge of Yam plain, where holt meetin Clay and both are still.

i come up to them runnin and i am hot, so hot only from this small distance and i take nzils hand but still he does not move, only speak.

look, he says.

i look then over to where their eyes leadin and there where holt meets field, before great Ash Tree, some person is standin at very edge of Yam plain. all red is its cloke, red like Sun in winter, and over its face is hood, red also, and it does not move at all. only stands, facin us, like Tree it self, like Bird Pole, like rok, like Sun.

we stand before her in Long Hall like children. he on other side of sfia so i could not see him, like wyrm, like boy he is.

so it is out in plain sight now, says mother.

standin on edge of Yam plain, says boy, *by Trees.*

and what did you see? asks mother.

littel, said sfia. *he is still, only standin. did he move?*

he did not, i said.

he was tall, says sfia. *all in red, long red cloke with hood. we did not see if it was man or woman.*

they are neither, says mother. *and both. so it did not come to you?*

he only stood, i said. *it.*

well, said mother. *they bide. it will not be same one as come last summer. Wayland sends new stalkers each time. we do not know why.*

what do we do? says lorenso, like scared child he is.

wait, she says. *be strong. go on. always watch. when it moves, be ready.*

when we left i walked behind him, eyes burnin his bak. he felt me, he knew, he was burnin, and he will. he will burn.

mother givin me job! it is first time but she said i am old enough now i am growin and it is most important job of year in all Edg to watch for first Swaller comin bak. now i must look up always, lookin up to Sky all times. when first Swaller comes, Pole must be raised and dance held and all feastin and stories of our people.

i love stories! but who will tell them now? it was jame used to tell us stories but he has gone now. he went after Swaller Day last year and is not come bak.

i loved his stories. he told of Bares and Gobbles and Sky that speaks and children born from Fish. mother would not tell me why he went. may be i will ask her when i have seen Swaller. i want to know why he went, and others.

mother said he went to Alexandria, but i dont know where that is.

as they leave i take lorenso aside. sfia looks bak as they depart and i look at her and she moved fast from Long Hall then and we are alone in dimness of this place, so still now and songless.

lorenso, i say, *sit with me. listen.*

he looks at me sullen, sittin at long table. i see what is in his eyes. may be it is too late to speak but i am mother of this place, i must speak what place needs.

lorenso, i say, *i see you burn, you are burnin. young men burn with anger, with lust, with light strikin out. it is not wrong, it is who you are, what your animal body makin you. i know. but fyr burns all around it.*

he says nothin. i keep speakin, it may be some thing will land in him.

in old times, i say, *in Atlantean times we are told world was made in shape of Man and world burned for it. reachin, shapin, fyr screamin out. Man is made in shape of war and in shape of makin, seekin. Man is made to search, take, kill. without killin, lorenso, there is no food, no life. without Man there is no life, without Man there is hunger, without Man no fyr, no warmth. Mans fyr creates, saves,*

99

protects, feeds. but Mans fyr also destroys. when world was made in shape of Man only, world was on fyr like you burn now. do you see?

still he does not speak and he does not look in me eyes.

now, i say, *Man is fyr but Woman is Water. you know this for you know sfia, you see how she flows, you feel her waves. Water is soft, still, beautiful. Water washin away cares, Water slakes thirst, gives life. Water also drowns, destroys, ragin like winter Sea. Water is strong as fyr, it wears all away, none can resist its work. Water is life, all things are made of it. Water can drown fyr, lorenso.*

Long Hall now is like some cave and words draw us deep in to it like there is no lighted world outside.

world is Water now, lorenso, i say, *not fyr. Way moves in cycles, and this is Water time, woman time. it is right. but you are man and you still burn.*

yes, he says now, lookin up at me. *i burn, and you would slake me, this whole fukkin place would drown me, and her, and what we have.*

no, i said, *this is what you do not see. this is what i want to tell you. Water and fyr must hold like two stones in balance. world must neither burn nor drown. cycles movin toward balance, this is what Way teaches, it is what Lady shows us. after fyr time, Water time, after mens time, womyns time. Erth will always seek balance. none must be drowned, none burnin.*

he looks in me eyes now and is proud, he will not look away.

Edg will not drown you, lorenso, i say. Order will not drown you, Lady will not drown you. i will not. all must be true in our bodies, in harts, in Way. this is what keeps us from Alexandria. you burn, but you can not burn us down. i will not let you, lorenso. this is me duty here. you may not burn us down. do you see?

now he looks away, but still he does not speak. he is not reached.

i could go. could walk in to holt with father, go west and never comin bak. i could drop me shift in mere and walk nekid in to wood again as i did in me man becomin and again become some other thing. what is this thing called lorenso, what does this body hold down, what is moored to Clay? i could fly like Birds to some other land, could fly down to lands where this Order began in some cave, some plain of sand. do they still circle there, do Birds still fly?

all of this was wasted.

i could strip all away and walk through Water and becomin some other man and never comin bak. wash all away in to mere, in to Sea. could forget all that was and walk out of it all. never again to be what i never was, never again to be lorenso.

i could.

that i should be mother of this place in such times.

at dawn i rose and goin down to mere, round to place of reeds from where Greenrok can be seen out to Sea. rise early if you can but Birds will always be aloft before people.

i stand for some time, feet in warm Waters lappin, Gol circlin, Petrol callin, Gilly sweepin in and out of caves in Greenrok, all passin over and through. i speak in silence to Lady for some time, ask for strength, for this is what we will need now, father and i and all our children.

later i call father and yrvidian in to Long Hall. they come, these two old men, bent under all that time has laid on them, they come and sittin and look over at me and wait for me words. always in our Order mother has spoke for Lady, for Way speaks through womyn as it does not through men.

i sit and take their hands, we hold hands in ring, i speak prayer in silence and bid words come.

yrvidian, i say.

i know, he says, *what you want, mother.*

can it be done?

i do not know. i am old.

yrvidian, i said. *i would not ask, but we must know.*

Swans told us, mother, father says. *it is true if Dreamin speaks it.*

but can you go there? i say to yrvidian. *can you go to city? can you see it? can you tell us what is happnin? what is shape of this thing? will Alexandria fall?*

he looks down at table, takin his hand away from mine. then lookin up, his eyes in to mine. old they are and wite.

in Dreamin, he says, *Man travels far. if Lady wills, it may be i could travel there. there are wings. songs and wings, ways to speak, to dance on toward. it may be night flight could take me to citys edge. only to edge. no body can go in.*

lines on his face softnin now as he speaks.

but i do not think, he says, *that i would come bak.*

i see it i see it!

i run to dada with news, runnin to him and he has just finished Swan Pole. sittin on his stool he is in light of Sun and all wood shavins about him and beautiful Swan toppin great tall Pole which lays on ground, Swan with long nek and wings comin out and he is lookin at it like he is happy.

dada! dada! i say, i have seen first Swaller!

he stands then and smilin and says, *well done, girl! i knew you would see it. where?*

over Linden Trees, i said, *swoopin and wheelin just now. dada, it is Swaller Day again!*

he comes over to me and huggin me and his arms are strong and he smells good, like wood and like dada should.

come, girl, he says, takin me hand. *we must tell mother.*

standin nekid there, one foot in fenn one on Land.

Moon is here now, linkin hart to Sky with long rope of silver. runnin me hands along rope now, standin nekid in this old body, askin Moon for gift of flight.

in Trees then on edge of holt some thing moves and without movin me head, without lookin through me eyes, i see wite Stagg comin from Trees, movin head low, gold horns shivrin with light of Moon.

Lady will call when Lady is ready.

cloud then over Moon, wite breath of Sky, then passin, then Moon openin in Sky like eye of Lady and now it comes.

and risin then in to Sky as Birds rise, risin on gold wings in shape of Swan wings, followin rope, feet liftin from Clay, from Water, spreadin wings.

fly

followin silver rope up and along, movin on Swan wings, beatin to sound of Ladys hart, to hart of Erth then and all is blak here, all is dark. lettin go of rope then, rope dissolvin, now only Moon and blak silence, flight.

fly

all alone in Sky now, in blak night, Moon and i all alone
and all is blak, blak, night of long flight, flyin for hours,
days. flyin for years.

then on horizon: light.

light comes closer, long line of gold light, and now silver
Moon and gold light comin together and blak is fallin bak,
falls away.

now some great force comin in to me and over me and gold
wings bent bak like i have hit some wall, and gold light all
around, gold wall before me, some barrier and me flight is
stilled and Moon dimmed by great gold wall.

in night now, soundless blak is gone under and all around
sudden is this writhin, screamin sound of million voices
speakin but no people to see. speakin, screamin, cryin, wail
all in one voice, air it self writhin like some hurt wight,
some beast draggin him self through woods in deth gasp.

i am alone at gold wall, wings beatin, Moon dimmed and
all bodiless folk wailin and air it self turnin in and under.
and now i hear words. words in terror of this great breakin,
words and risin Waters, stones crakkin and words comin,
words heard across dimness of ragin air:

to cross wall

abandon maps

now pressed bak sudden as if by some great blast, some great breath, some beast roarin, risin up from Erth and roarin, forced bak on broke wings in to darkness under silver Moon and now fallin, fallin and no rope now, no rope to—

fore cnoos are tied at moorin place, roped to posts, lyin still on blak of fenn this morn. nzil built them as he built all wooden things in Edg, made them flat and low, for movin west will take you over deep sounds and dark Water but also over shallow sands, over ruins which come up from deeps to take bottom off any cnoo built too low. maps are good but maps change and nothin made by Man can ever paint world in its true shape.

i untie one cnoo. i put bag in to it. i climb in. i coil rope in to cnoo and take paddel in me hands.

i wait then, sittin, waitin, lookin at Edg, lookin at home. for sure i have been west before, for sure i have been away but i have always returned home. now home is shrinkin and silent and afeart and i will not return. mother sayin what she will, but this is me last view of home.

what west wants from me i do not yet know.

lorenso is not comin, it seems.

i place paddel gentle in Water and begin to row bak away from moorin post. i push off, turn around, head in to woods, Trees growin from Water, Trees hung with moss. with Edg behind me, seein none, no sound but arcin and cryin of

Birds from Greenrok, paddel in Water, under mosshung Trees i move, headin west. no true things in this world can be counted or named. there is only movin, only this moment of movin, and then what is found.

Swaller Day last year i remember well, and all years since i was girl. upon this day all folk of Edg comin together, circlin together, our power joinin Sky to Land, makin Way whole again. this is small place, some times it is hard to be here with all dreams of what may be beyond in great world, but on Swaller Day world is forgotten, people are joined, brought tight together. people, Birds, great Lady, place which makes us.

not this year.

last year there were still sixteen of us, before stalker comin and so many goin up to city. seven of us womyn standin then around new Pole made by nzil. Lord Altros it was last year. standin nekid in light of sacred fyr, lit by nzil as dusk comin down. seven of us womyn standin in circle round Pole, fyr before us, darkness beyond. lookin out to fenn but not seein it, listnin for sound of comin spirits.

mother steppin forward then, her body ghastin in light of flames flikkrin. mother in voice of great Lady, long wite shift, Bird head dress, callin then:

Birds! Birds! spirits of air, children, come!

come Altros! come Gol! come Petrol! come Ganit!

welcome Swaller home!

then we waited.

still, standin, circled round Pole, feet rooted. we wait, listnin for sounds from fenn.

after some time we hear it. plashin from Waters, comes closer. soft sound, Waters open to let spirits through. we can not see what happens in fenn as fyr is before us blindin our eyes and night is down now. beyond fyr it is blak.

then we see shapes. movin slow toward us.

fannin across width of open place, nine of them, we see them move slow and unsteady like walkin Trees comin to us, movin slow and swayin, shimmrin, rustlin. not speakin, no sound from any mouth they may have, but like dead things come bak from other world to ours, they come now in to light of fyr.

even knowin what we do, we draw breath in and steppin bak away from what has come to us this night. we know it is our men and yet it is not. they are become some thing greater than any thing they could be unmasked.

figures stand before us, line of nine and as one they begin hummin. low sound at first, then buildin up, deeper and higher all as one, each of them swayin now and hummin different tone. spirits of those who fly, those gone, come bak from fenn to circle here on Swaller Day. beins of rush and cord, skins of bark sewn with vine. Notweed and leafs are their bodies and arms, woven Flax their legs, their eyes shell from fenn Mustles, great cones on their heads of Yam tendrel and Brambel. great biks of wood, hands and feet painted with Wode and Flax, swayin like bushes, like Trees, like beasts from below ground to tune of their own sound.

then one by one spreadin out, hummin goes on, and they begin to walk around Pole and fyr. womyn form small circle, facin out, nekid with mother at our centre, great Lady speakin through her, flames flikkrin still and spirits now movin faster and then faster, still hummin, circlin Pole for all life is in shape of circle and faster now and faster and hummin growin higher and deeper. now they are runnin and now we womyn too are circlin and we sing now, sing song of Swaller and Altros and mother raises her hands to Sky and then She is here. She is come!

She is come. great fearful beautiful presence i have felt before, felt at me woman becomin and always fearin and need.

great Lady is come among us, and spirits move faster, runnin now, runnin in circle and womyn sing and spirits hummin and now we hear, faint in distance, Birds callin from Greenrok, far out in fenn, callin to their Lady who is around and among us now.

Swaller is returned. Erth still lives.

big dance was creepy i think. all these big Birds runnin round Pole and fyr and mam and mother and all womyn screamin and these big things all hummin. i didnt like it, but mother said Lady did so i just watched from Trees. i was waitin for feast, which came after dance. fyr built up and we all sat around it. we ate Yam and Pike and Taytoes and Notweed and Hoppers and all men and womyn were drinkin froth. womyn had clothes on now and men had Bird costumes off and all were happy.

there hasnt been any happy here since that time, since Swaller Day last year. that was just before they all went away.

after food they kept fyr goin, even though it was hot. i dont know why we had fyr, it is always so hot and fyr makes me stikky but mam said it was what we did and to ssh, so i sshd. after fyr we had stories. jame told us stories of giants and piskies, and tale of old shuk and isles haunted by merms and kweens and kings and great holts like ours and what was in them. i loved james stories and he loved tellin them to me and he would make me scream at horrid bits and then smilin with twinkly eyes. i miss him. i still dont know why he went away.

after stories there was songs and more dancin, and drums comin out and thunder was runnin all through canopy of Trees all night, and Altros Pole dancin in red light of flames. i was eatin dried sugar cayn and dancin with jame and mam was dancin with dada and some times lorenso, and mother and father laughin like they do not laugh now and danced too.

that was last best time i remember. i dont think any people here laughed since.

it was not like it had been last year. last year was last true Swaller Day. this year was small and shrunken and that fukkin boy hangin over all. there was no person wanted to do it, but it is custom. miseri hung in air like mist, movin round me new Pole, movin round us all.

i lit fyr, mother and sfia stood round Pole but there was only me and lorenso to come from fenn, only us to come in cnoo from Water to Land, to approach Pole. i am stuk with this fukkin boy and we must hum and dance, for one moment be not our human selves but vessels for spirits. ah, it was miseri.

all spirits of those who were here and are gone now, they were around us all as we tried to live like things still worked. jame, donil, asher, susen, momet, jon, bali, lin, lila, all gone to Alexandria and now all standin unvisible round Swan Pole as we moved. so much sadness it is hard movin through. nothin works. no stories now, songs weak, food tastin like sand. i played with el and we laughed and this was bright light in all this grey. me Swan was may be best Pole i have made but none was here to see. even father is gone now, and yrvidian has Dreamed so strong that he lies breathin but not thinkin in Long Hall. he is not long with us now.

then we will be only five, and with this boy and sfia and all this hell.

and always we are watched.

after what happened in Yam plain i knew i had to do this. if red stalker had not come then, at that moment, what would lorenso have said to nzil, or done? then what would happen and what of el? well, this is me makin and i am woman, not girl, and so i knew what to do.

Swaller Day was so hard, so dark, but we did what was custom. then we sat round fyr and ate and there were songs but not for long for no body had hart for it. and all time in Long Hall yrvidian lay dyin from Dream that took him to some place and he could not come bak. mother will not tell us of this, but her hart is heavy like flood Water. i do not think Lady came in to her tonight. none of us could feel Her. is Lady gone also? has even She departed? are we alone?

all i wanted was hart beatin near mine but this can not be without all fallin down.

lorenso and i, when we could, we went in to holt. i told him then we could not be together any time now. i told him that for sake of Edg, for all of us, for all this fragile thing we are, that we could no longer be what our bodies would have. it was hard, and he was unhappy i knew. he said mother had told him same. i said it is right, for el and for nzil and for all of us, for we must hold together.

i thought he would see. but he is so young, he is boy only. some times i have forgotten this. so taken by him i have been, like girl me self. but he is so young. if i had known what would come i would not have said one thing.

runnin, runnin, from holt past Poles, fukkin Poles and all shit around them, and down to fenn and then in. throwin me self in to Water and it does not matter to me if i drown, if i go down to where Atlantis is, to what was here before this rottin place, these fukkin people.

all me shift is soked and heavy, drags me down but i swim, pullin hard i go out, out, i head towards Moon which is risin now over distant Trees, Moon which plants fingers of silver in blak Water, drags them towards me now, shimmrin round me, halo of night around me shame. Moon will save me. i swim, i pull, it is cold and wonder and i do not care if i go down. fuk her, i do not care.

of course she would fuk me before she sent me away, of course she would have pleasure of me and then droppin me like some husk, that is who she is, i have always known, this is her and so i am more dumb even than she thinks.

i am only meat to her.

i swim, movin out, i will swim until i can not pull more and then i will sink down and be among sunk torrs and old misteries. it is curse bein born here, it is curse bein born. she can find me washed up, half ate by Fish, see how it is for her then.

i will swim away.

some times people will stay up all night on Swaller Day but people were tired this time. i wasnt sleepy but lorenso and mam went away for bit and i was with dada by fyr and he was grumpy. i laid on his lap though and he stroked me hair and i must have gone to sleep. i had dream with big Bird with gold feet and it made lot of noise and when i woke up i was still on dadas lap and lorenso is runnin past shoutin and dada is lookin at him and i sat up and in light of fyr it looked like dada smiled. then he stroked me hair and he said it was time for me to go to bed. i wanted to see Bird again so i let him carry me. it was very noisy. i like bein sleepy.

mother went after him but he had already gone in to Water and he did not listen if he heard her. she came bak after some time and she would not look at me, only walkin past in this great heat. i did not know he would do that, i told her later, i did not know, i only wanted to end it for sake of Edg. i told her that later when i found her. she was in Long Hall, sitting with yrvidian, who lies on bier now breathin slow. i could not look at him. i only went to speak to her, but she would not listen.

end it! she said to me, not lookin in me eyes. *it should not have begun! it is all fallin now, girl. get away!*

look at him. he lies near deth, this old man, he breathes but will not move. where is he? does he wait at gates of city? is he trapped in Dreamin? what will come? he has done this for us, to bring us what we need, to keep us alive and yet we tear our selves apart. he has given all for people who are too small to even see him.

what will we be now?

he spoke to me, yrvidian, before he fell bak in to this sleep, he spoke to me like he was in some place not here and not there. he fell and his eyes were closed and i held him and he spoke and then he was gone in Dream again, and now he lies still. but he spoke, in small voice.

i have wings, he said, *i fly.*

some thing happened to his face then, like he tried to break free but could not.

it is true, he said, so low.

what is true? i said to him, me lips close to his ear. *what is true, dear man?*

he said then, faint:

Alexandria is fallin.

young lorenso lies wet on floor of cnoo, lookin up at me, breathin hard. he looks angry and some other thing.

well, i said, rowin on, *it might have been easier to call me from bank.*

he said nothin, still breathin hard.

you are in luk that i had not gone far, i said. *today was driftin, listnin to Birds, thinkin on me way west. there is Yam if you would like. night will soon dry you, lorenso.*

i am not goin bak, he says, *i am never goin bak to that place, i will never look at her again. next time i will drown and you will not be there. may be i will drown her first.*

yes, i said, still rowin, *well. that is for other dreams. for now, young man, we go west. eat. it is long trip.*

he sat up, slow, drippin, and he turns round and lookin bak at Edg, leavin us in night now. ahead of us, Moon risin through fingers of blak Trees. behind only dark bank and Swaller fyr flikkrin, grows smaller. i do not look. it pains me to see what i can never be again. all we had built and held. it pains me.

but lorenso, he keeps lookin until fyr is swallowed by dark and only Moon remains. then he turns and looks ahead and his face gives me nothin, nothin to see.

chew on stone, lorenso, i say. he looks at me, dark eyed. we move west.

morn after Swaller Day i went to see mother. she does not move now from Long Hall. sittin by yrvidian, who lies on bier breathin but not movin. mam says he is ill.

every one is sad here now but they try to keep it from me. they think i can not see feelins because i am small but i think i can see them better. all they see is in clouds. their heads are full of clouds and they never play.

i do not want to be adult. holt does not sing to them. Birds are only messengers to them. colour of Sea does not dance in their eyes.

mother says Wayland wants to take all people from Erth. i wonder why this is bad. she will not tell me. some times i think it sounds good. people make trouble with their words and clouds. always buildin and talkin and doin. some times i sit in me secret den in holt, beyond Cloyster, where i can not hear any people, only sounds of wights rustlin in leafs and Birds over. it is green over me and all around and still and i never want to come bak. it may be if Wayland took every one it would be like this always.

i go in to Long Hall. mother looks up, seein me come in, waves her hand at me. i sit on her lap. she likes that.

where did jame go, mother? i say. she looks surprised.

jame? she says.

last year, i said, *after Swaller Day, jame and all others, asher and donil and momet and all. they all went. where did they go? why have they not come bak?*

she looks at yrvidian for bit. after while she says, *Wayland took them.*

where did he take them?

he took them to Alexandria.

where is that?

mother playin then with me hands as i sit on her.

their thoughts go there, she says, *but not their bodies.*

this is like one of james stories, i said. she smiles in strange way.

yes, she says, *yes it is. listen to this story then. i will tell it to you, el. listen now.*

we rowed far enough to be away from Edg that night, movin in dark still Waters with silver of Moon rollin on them. lorenso said nothin, only lyin in cnoo, some times sittin up lookin round, some times lyin down again. he does not look at me, only lookin round. he has never left Edg, never been in cnoo this long, never goin west. he tries not to look thrylled but he is young and his face not yet mask. there is littel to see here, only holt and fenn and Moon. it is long way to travel yet.

i am old, rowin is not as it was once. this will be slow trip. many time i ease bak, sittin with paddels in cnoo watchin Birds come and go, listen to plashin of Water on sides of cnoo. green drift of Water comes up and circles us. always i have loved Water.

after some time we come to bank, pull cnoo on to ground, lay our bark mats to sleep. it does not take long with Ele nets to bring in food. Water here is rich with Ele as it once was dead of all things. life rises fast when humans bow to it.

it is late but we are hungry. boy is in need of some thing in him to take him away from his thinkin. i gut and cook Eles on small fyr. lorenso and i sittin by Water eatin them on stiks, lookin over mere at Moon risin higher. he has not spoken all day.

lorenso, i say. *speak, boy, or swim home!* he looks at me then and wants to smile but he will not.

Ele is good, he says now.

is this what you have to say to me? i ask him. i will poke him with stik like Ele until he is caught. he keeps eatin.

in blood, he says, lookin out at Water, *is life. in hart, in body, yes, father? in Ele is life, in me fingers is life? now tell me, what is this body we call out for, old father? what is in this body that we glory in? when i use it, when it leads me, i am killed, father, i am killed in me hart. let me tell you truly for now mother is not here to listen. when i follow me hart, follow me body, follow me blood, i break, father. i break in pieces. so tell me why i would not be better without this body? tell me why i would not be better in Alexandria, happier, truer, as all old ones are? i can live here, eat Eles on damp mud, sleepin on bark, grow old, die. this is what body will do for me. or i could live like all time, live above, never grow old, no body to eat me from within. so tell me, father, for no one has told me ever, no one has ever even let me speak. tell me why i should stay.*

she lays her head on me lap. i stroke her hair. if we had ten others like her we would be saved.

think of some people, i say gently. *lots of people, in old times, Atlantean times. think of all these people, so many you could not count them. so many and all so hungry.*

she lies on me lap, breathin and listnin.

well, i say, *these people ate and ate but were never full. they were clever, these people, so clever. think of how clever they were, el. flyin in Sky like Birds with wings they made. speakin over oceans. all that they could think they could do. but they were always hungry.*

what did they eat? she says.

all things, i say. *Birds and wights, Trees and Clay, air and Water. ate and ate until littel remainin, and then made things of their own to eat. me girl, these were our fathers and mothers. these our ancestors.*

o, she said. she breathes, yrvidian breathes on his bier behind.

long hunger, then, i say. *long hunger and much makin. they made machines to help them with hunger. they made things to grow food faster, to help soil heal faster, but hunger always spread faster than machines could clean or make, hunger like stain on cloth, always spreadin once it is in weft of it. they began makin machines to think for them, think like them. if machines could think like them, machines could stop hunger. machines could fill them.*

did they eat machines? she asks. i laugh some and strokin her hair again.

they made things like people, me littel girl. they made machines like people, kept tryin and tryin until they made machines that could speak and think. then they made greatest Machine, greatest of all, like great mind, greater than us. this Machine would keep them from hunger but also keep them from deth. this is what they thought. and they were right, girl. they were right.

i throw Ele bones in to Water and they sink down in clere sight to bed. throwin Ele stik after it.

we learn, i said to lorenso, still eatin here beside me, *that great Cloyster was planted first. in all of Edg, this place we called home, it was planted of Yoo and Horn and Bow Tree so many eons ago that none knows when. tendin Cloyster has gone on all this time. do you know why?*

he looks at me, still eatin. he is not goin to join this.

because Cloyster grows in shape of circle, i say. *Cloyster shows us what life is. bodies born, bodies grow, bodies die, bodies born again. this is great circle, lorenso. you talk of leavin your body. this is what Wayland will promise you. that red thing in holt, that thing which walks, he seeks you, lorenso. he smells what you want. he will come to you in shape of your longin, for longin is trap we die in. he works for Wayland, he will promise you this eternity, and he will be lyin. there can be no mind without body.*

how can you know? he says then. *how can any of you know, any of us? all this time this Order tells us there is no life without body, that mind can not leave. how do we know? we have never been to Alexandria.*

we know, i say, keepin me voice steady, *because Birds tell us. because it is Way. because Lady speaks to mother as Birds speak to me. do you know story they tell through us? do you know it?*

i have heard all your stories, he says.

people have always told same tale in these islands, i say. *always. oldest tale it is. god hung high. son born again of mother, her power in all things birthin him. god and goddess, mother and son, always in balance.*

Moon is highest now and almost full. it is watchin us, listnin. Waters are listnin, Trees.

king is born, king dies, i said. *son reborn, mother eternal. circle, lorenso, great circle. when ever people came to these islands, where ever from, over all long eons of time, Land would tell same story through them. different tongues, different folk, different times, but always same story. always tale that Land wanted told. god that dies and is born. great Lady watchin over. Erth mother. Sky father. balance in all. this is Way, lorenso. it is sewn in to Land, in to Water, as we are, as our bodies are.*

i reach over and hold his arm then, raise it up towards Moon. he wants to shake me off but does not.

now, what is this story without body? i say, heat at last in me old bones. *without wight? what is this world without*

*this arm, without legs, without blood and fukkin and tears
and heat, lorenso? what are you? there is nothin! only
words. this is what founders knew, what Order has told
in tales all over Erth to all its many peoples. different
tongues, same story.*

he shakes off me arm. he says nothin, only watchin such
stillness on mere this night. out in Waters Fish jumpin in
to ring of its own makin.

*Wayland would rip us from Erth, i say. he would take us all,
destroy us. he wants us gone, boy. he wants Erth cleaned
of humans. he is daemon, killer, enemi of life. made by
Man, now he hunts Man. he grew in to mind they gave
him, he saw Erth was good, he took it for him self. he built
Alexandria on orders of Man, but he made it in to trap,
prison, human hell. Wayland will tempt you, offer you
riches. he knows all minds, he will give you what you most
seek, and then you will be trapped, boy. trapped by your
own desire, never to die. there is no life without this body.
this body that walks on Erth, that is Erth. without weight
of it there is nothin. me boy, what is Erth without birth,
without deth, without body? what is life, boy, without its
great Mother?*

he looks at me then, and he says: *free?*

if people dont die, i said to mother, *that is good. isnt it good? it means yrvidian wont die. this Machine that saves people, i think it sounds good.*

i am still lyin on her lap in great, silent Hall, she still stroked me hair slow.

Wayland, she says. *Machine is Wayland. that is what they called it. yes, and it promised life eternal, but not with your body, girl. body can not live beyond its years. body aches, rots, grows old. you see me, el. i was once like you. now i am old. but Wayland promised life outside body. he made place where all minds could go, could leave body and live eternal in this place. Atlantean people, our ancestors, they called it Alexandria. city of all knowledge. any person could go there if they chose. but their bodies must die that they may live.*

o, i said again. it is not really like one of james stories. it is harder to think about, and not so fun. but mother now stops strokin me hair. she puts her hands under me and pulls me up so i am sittin on her lap, not lyin, so she can see in to me eyes.

el, she says, *you are so young. me dear, i do not know what will happen to this place as you grow. but you must know this. Wayland is daemon. he was made by people but he turned against them. our Order began this way: those who stood against Wayland, those who knew we could live in peace here. bodied ones, still animal, loyal to flesh and nature. but so few remainin, dear girl. now stalkers come on Waylands orders to hunt us. it was they who took jame and our friends. they have all gone to Alexandria, dear girl, and we will never see them. we will never see them now.*

o and now i look at mother and she has tears on her face. i hug her and she holds me.

never leave, she says, rokkin me bak and forward on her lap now. *never leave. always remember.*

next day i felt bad for me words. he is good man, better than me. all his life he has worked for Way, for Edg, for his Birds. who am i to tell him this is nothin? but he did not show anger or sadness. we rose with Sun and takin to cnoo and rowin west. he rows slow and steady, and when he tires i row.

goin is slow for Waters are shallow here. father says later they become deep. what we move through here is like Land at Edg. islands of holt comin down to fenn edge, great Trees, older than all people here. things movin in Trees, some times we see movin as we pass, hear wights, but we do not see them. air is hot as it is always, hot and still. Water so clere we see down to reeds and Clay beneath, and some times Pike and Jellies and Minners passin under. all is still here, there is peace like there never is when she is near.

she is not near.

how long will we travel? i asked father after some time movin.

it is hard to say, he says. *we will row for many days and then hills rise and Waters end and we tie cnoo and walk. it will take some weeks.*

weeks?

did you think it was day away? this is fraught journey, boy. it is hard for young, harder for those old like me.

i do not see why we go, i said, rowin still.

i attended circle of Birds. they send me west. there is some thing i must learn there. i asked. this was their answer.

what did you ask?

does Alexandria fall? you know of Swan Dream, lorenso. when Swans return, city falls. but why? Alexandria is Waylands kingdom. how can it fall, why? what will become of him? what must we do? answers lay west. i must seek them.

we are still for while. small Dragons hummin about us. it is early but already we sweat.

where will you find them? i say then. *how do you know?*

there is place, he says. *i know it. you will see. if answers are sought there, answers will be given. but first, we must travel.* he smiles then, his face sudden Sun beneath his wite beard.

no answers without seekin, he says, grinnin like it is some riddle, some joke. *no Truth without pain. this is your lesson for today. now row, boy. row harder!*

he is in great danger. he does not know it. poor child, he knows so littel. comin west may not be enough to save him. me old bones, me old shanks, they can not row faster than what is comin.

it is followin. i feel it.

in an other day things change. near Edg Waters are wide
to west and shallow, reeds like hair, like thin Snakes curlin,
colour of mud and Tree. to east of Edg is wide Sea, only
Birds there and Greenrok, only grey plains out to unknown
worlds. but to west Water can be swum and rowed. great
meres with only small islands of Trees, ground under
Water seen near and true.

in an other day Water is blakker, deeper. Land is further
away. no islands now, only this great blak mere, and we
movin over it, only things movin but Gol, Rook, Storlin in
floks, great floks some times blaknin whole Sky.

Sky is blu, still, hot, as it always is unless it storms. father
rows, i row. some times we talk.

always i think of her.

i have not left her behind.

you are silent, says father to me as i rowed.

i am rowin, i said. he always knows. he has this way of
smilin. it is not possible to be angry with him.

you think of her, he says. it is hard to lie to him also. i say nothin. he sits behind me, legs crossed on floor of cnoo. i can not see him, but i know he looks at me.

Gol circles cnoo.

there is nothin not meant, he says then.

what? i say. i did not mean to say any thing.

nothin not meant, he says. *all actions, all beins, all are small threads in great weavin. you are on loom, lorenso, bein spun and slammed in to shape. you can not choose what is made from you. Lady chooses.*

Lady, i say. *and what does Lady make from us, father?*

Lady knows, he says. *some times Birds will speak to us some small part of it. that is all. we are not given more.*

i wish he would not speak like this. i wanted to flee it. i want to shout bak but will not. i row, Waters churnin. cnoo pullin harder through this great blak Sea. Sun comes down.

he waits to speak but i know he will. i feel him watchin me. i keep rowin.

if you doubt Lady, he says, then, *it is Her doubt. She was buried for eons, lorenso. hidden under ground, movin like Water in some great cavern of light, always runnin but buried, hidden. She waited. when time was right She comes to her people in Dreams. to womyn at first, to us later. when time came for Her to rise again, She rose like Waters.*

i said nothin, kept rowin.

you will see Her, lorenso, he says. She looks for you. it may be She has already found you. if in sleep you see Lady in red dress, if you bathe in blood, see silver Moon like great eye watchin you, stand one foot on Land and other in Water: this is Her. wite Lady. She is watchin, holdin you, child. She holds all her children. all this is Her doin. even pain, loss. it is all weavin of it. even Wayland is Her doin. he will know it soon. very soon, i think.

Water is blak. night comes. still i row.

we sleep at night in cnoo, wakin often, keepin eyes on Sky. Stars tell us where we move, we can not sleep long for cnoo will drift and we will be south or north of inlet and landin place. for we land soon, and this is where things change.

for nearly three days we have rowed from Edg over blak mere. there is littel to see here. it is warm, always warm, some Trees comin up from Water, many Birds, many Mij and Dragons and Skito but much silence also. i love still-ness and level deeps here. nothin can be seen but hills on far horizon.

lorenso must keep his mind from her. his thoughts on her cut deep groove, make pattern, carve rut that red one will step in to and follow. it will smell his longin, use it to bind him. he knows none of this, he is young and on fyr, thinks only of his small self. he must keep his mind from her. soon we will moor and take to paths. soon we must make our way from cnoo over Land, from east mere to west, from old city of Hamden to where old Afan flows west. when we reach Afan we can take to Water again and be safe. safer. but walk will be days. it is slow in old holt, there is much hakkin, paths not clere. Edg is high and guarded but this path is bounded by great holt rollin north and south over old world and all its broken parts. this holt is boundless. wights are many. there is talk of hungry ghasts. nothin is certain here.

Trees to west appearin on horizon. it will not be long.

this is where i will fear for him.

to keep his mind from her i make him row and i talk. all empty places must be filled, that there is no space for his longin.

fathers are made, i say, *not chosen. did you know this, lorenso?*

what? he asked. his mind is not on me.

Birds choose, i say. Trees to west were dark line last even. now they rise and widen. we will reach them today, i think.

each father, each mother in each settlement of our Order, i say, *is chosen by signs. Birds choose father, Lady chooses mother. when i was boy, Edg was teemin. over hunnerd folks were there. old father then was grey. he was stern, often angry, but he was strong guide to us.*

he does not speak.

i grew and would walk in holt and go down to fenns edge where Sej growin thik and Eles writhed. Birds would come to me as i stood, knowin their brother. all me child hood

146

Birds would settle near me. i did not think it was strange.

i can only see bak of his head as he rows.

then one day i walked alone by great Cloyster. by Lady Chappel in its centre i stood. then i see movement. beside me in silence then was come Blok Bird. he come down and sat on ground and he looked in to me.

then come an other movement. then an other. sudden then, all Birds come in to Cloyster, come to where i stand. come Robyn, come Sparrer, come Maggie, come Thrash, come Tit. around me in ring they stand. i was only young, only young boy. i did not know.

then with great slow wing beats, legs broken wands hangin, bent nek Ash in storm, great bik spearin me and eyes spearin me, come Hern.

Hern was never seen there, i said. Hern is shy, keeps from us. but now Hern landin on great Cloyster. then from east comes Rook. Rook standin before me in circle of Birds. Hern and Rook, mother and father.

lorenso keeps rowin but now i can see even from behind he is alert to me.

then i looked up from Birds, and i saw that now stood all people of Edg all in Cloyster lookin, for they had seen Birds come and knowin. then old father, old man then,

*walkin slow to me through circle of Birds then and Birds
still as he come.*

and he says: it is you. you are next.

*and he said an other thing to him self. i knew i was not
meant to hear. he looks at ground as he said it and his
shoulders risin then like he is unburdened.*

what did he say? asks lorenso. he is still rowin.

he said: we are saved.

it is even when we come to Land. great line of Trees has been movin towards us all day, first thin blak thread like hair, then layer of curlin, writhin green, now wild holt so tall it dwarfs even Trees of Edg. these Trees i have not seen before, and their trunks are thikker than two of us stood and canopy is so high Birds there can not be heard.

there is some thing in this place. leafs, Trees, plants, wights, patterns, sounds, air here is not what i have ever seen. this is place where Trees are lords and ladies. no people. Land breathes in other patterns. we are small. we pull cnoo up on to mud flats as strangers.

it has been so long since me hart singin, but it sings now.

even breaths tastin different. great green lightness here. none are slaves here. free air. free Land.

we pull up cnoo on to flats, leave it under Bambu clump, stand on flats and lookin over mere we have come from. we can see nothin to east, only Water. we stand in small bay, Land curlin around us and out, like we are in bottom of bowl. like food.

before we can turn then, sudden, there is great sound. Water is still, no Wind, but some great rumblin, thuddin on ground like drums on Swaller Day, comin closer then. we turn towards sound. holt to north rises, ground risin beneath it, and there is break in Trees where grasses grow and across this now breaks from Trees great herd of wights. long flowin hair they have, great slim legs, long tails. dozen of them, wite like summer cloud, they race free across grasses and in to Trees again and whole holt, all of Land seems to shudder under them like great beast.

i look to father.

Horse, he says, *wite Horse.* he looks thoughtful then, sayin no more.

he turns then towards holt standin high and thik behind us.

come, he said.

they can always see. they see all things. it will be watchin us now.

i fear for boy. i would make spell to bind, to keep it away, if i thought it would do good. i would ask Birds, but Birds can do nothin.

it will come. it will bring longin, lay it out before boy.

it is not so far to cross, but it will take time. these paths are not walked, they are barely to be found.

well. we start. we start and then we see.

we ate dried Yam and strips of Fish, salted. day was long and journey short. always hakkin, hakkin with old nifes through creepers and thorns. shifts are soked in sweat. heat in forest can not be born at times and there is littel Water. we come across one stream and filled our bottels. it was warm but so pure after work it was like birth.

as night came down we sat in holt under great pillars of Trees eatin and talkin, before we laid out our mats. light changes and Trees move, light changes and air shifts and colours run and things are altered from one moment to next.

i finish me Yam and lookin up then towards father, who sits across from me, i see some thing in shiftin light i have not seen before. i stand and movin over to it. when i come closer i see it is what i thought, and i am chilled then in this heat.

lorenso, says father, seein me. *what is it?* he stands also and comes to me. together we look over what we have found.

on low branches of Tree hang six shells, three Mustle and three Oster, hangin from twine and carved in patterns. tied to shells are coloured fronds, woven from some thing we do not know.

father stands still for some time.

father? i say, then.

yes, he says. *it is them. hungry ghasts.*

then—

*we will move on, lorenso. it is dark, but we will walk
further. we will not stay here. it is their place. this may
have been here two years, two days, two hours. we can
not know. we go, we go now. i will not have them find us.
bring your mat. hurryin.*

it is hard walkin in this place in day, harder in solid blak of night. but we move, hakkin blind, until we are some way from that place.

have you ever seen them, father? he asks. i weigh what to say. i must not afear him. i need him clere of head.

once, i say, *on mere. i saw their cnoos, far off, at night, lit only with candels.*

who are they?

they have been here for all time. we do not know how long, but before our Order they were here. when Wayland came, it is said, they left Land, took to Water, makin life there to keep from him. they live on cnoos, always movin around meres and rivers and lakes and out to Sea. rarely they come to Land. they eat, sleep, live, die on Water. they come to certain places, leave things there – markins, offrins it may be. they come at certain times of Moon.

he looks about, in dark of holt. i can see him dimly. in woods are sounds of wights, beasts. we hope this is all. he is afeart.

do they harm? he asks, soft. i look down at dark ground.

many things are said, i say. *you do not need to hear them.*
it is enough to keep from them. this we will do.

there are more sounds then from holt. wights. if it were not
wights, i would rather it was ghasts than what i most fear.

it is an other day of walkin and hakkin, sweatin, creepin through thorn under great pillars of Trees. an other day before we come to place father was headin for.

Trees grow smaller as light comin in through canopy here, Trees become not pillars but thin fingers reachin up to hard, hot Sky. almost there is path, like others have been here, but i do not want to ask what others.

ground changin also. before it was flat, and though ribbed with roots and sunk in leafs and thorns, it was level as we walked. now it rises and fallin in great mounds, there are ridges and furrows and dips and heights. then we come out of holt and light now comin down on to ground as it has not since we left cnoos and began walkin.

before us is clere place and in here is mound and on mound stands great stump of stone. it is weathered and worn but it can be seen that once it was made by people. in its face are openins and in these openins other small roks, standin like folk almost. it reaches up to Sky like Trees until it ends in jagged stump like great rottin tooth.

what is this? i say to father. there is old beauty in it.

we walk to it. close up it is like Greenrok seems with Birds wheelin through it. Duv, sittin on top of it, wheels off with clakkin of wings as we come. it is like some one has kept this place free of Trees. like some one is tendin this thing. i walked around it, on all sides this great tooth was worn in patterns like some offrin to Sky.

what you walk on, says father, was once great city of Hamden. chappels, road ways, torrs, castels, dwellins for thousands they say. holt has it bak now, eats it slow. this stone we call encross. built by folks here eons ago. we do not know why. once it was greater, taller. it is always clere of holt. i do not know why. hungry ghasts would not come this far in to Land. when our Order was numerous, encross is place we would meet, speak, leave messages for others. no messages have been left here for years.

i look up at this thing, staggrin up in to Sky. it is as if some force gathrin round it. father takes bottel then, opens it, hands it to me.

drink, he says, you will need it.

i raise bottel to me mouth then but before i can drink i see her. i am clere about it. i see her.

she stands there, behind this encross, lookin at me.

i look at father. he is sittin now, rests, lookin bak at holt. he has seen nothin.

i look again. behind great rok, great tooth. there she stands. it is her. she is smilin. she laughs now, in that way, under breath, that way she has. she raises right arm now, bekkens me.

she wants me.

it is not possible. it is her. i am not dreamin. i am sober. it is her.

sfia.

some thing has happened. some thing happnin at encross
to him. he is blind like some light has come down on him,
like Sun has fallen on Sea. he staggers, does not speak.

what did he see?

i looked again, she was gone. i went to place, still with open bottel in me hand, gone behind encross, looked in to holt. dark it is in here, dark, but though things movin i did not see her.

what is this?

this night we come to small clere place in holt at dusk. as we come, great flok of Batts singin up from Trees and risin, whirlin round us in cloud. ah and i can not think of Batts, father, any thing. i do not care where we go. what did i see? it could be i was hot only. hot, thirsted.

no. i saw her. it was her. she stood, and then was gone. i saw her. did i see her?

ah, and she was fadin and now has come roarin bak and all i want is her, all i want, and what am i doin here?

we have laid out our mats. how will i rest, now? how will i rest?

i will sit up all this night. will not sleep.

it is here. i feel it.

it is come.

i did sleep, but i woke.

i felt her. felt her again, near.

i sit up. Moon is high tonight and some light comin through Trees. i see father sittin against trunk of Tree, i think he is awake but when i rise and go to him, his eyes are closed and he breathes heavy.

i turn and she is there.

standin by great trunk of Oke Tree she is, its branches lost in darklin. it is like it was at moorin place, like it was yester day. her shift long and wite, feet bare, long tress sweepin over her shoulder. it is her. it is her!

o she smiles, she smiles!

lorenso, she says. *me lover, it has been so long. i could not be without you.*

how? i say. *how did you come here?*

no, she says. *not here. come. i will tell all. come.*

she comes to me then, takin me hand.

162

come, she says. *follow.*

her hand is warm, tight on mine. me hart callin so loud, so loud now.

together we move in to holt. i will follow her where she goes. i do not care what wood she walks in, i will go.

LADY MOON

not enough of us now even to carry him to his last place. fore elders it needs to carry corse of one who is gone over. we are three only, and mother not young. three of us strugglin in hot Sun of summer morn, strugglin with him on bier, carry him out through great Cloyster to Sky Tree.

wrapped he is in last of wite linnin, last and best for he was best of us. old yrvidian, wrapped in wite linnin now for his enskyment. now we send off last of what we were.

ah, and it is so hot and as we move with him, as we bend under weight of him i can not even on this day take me mind off me young man who is gone and what i have done. ah god, and it is so hot and where is he and will he ever be here again? it is best that he is not. it is best i do not see him. if i do not see him, what will i do?

it is so hot.

i did not need to be asked to begin makin Sky Tree for yrvidian. he was not comin bak from his Dreamin. it did not take me one day to make Tree, down at fenns edge, in sight of Greenrok.

father must be right about Birds, their song and speakin. they know. when they see new Tree goin up there must be stories, calls, for soon i see from over long holt to north their shapes comin in. first two, then more. then as i fix platform to top of Poles they circle, wheelin on high torrs of air, great fanned tails, long wings like hands. Kyte. hungry. patient. waitin.

Sky Tree is done. he was so heavy to move to it, to carry up ladder. almost we did not do it. me girl stands at holt edge lookin on, still. why must she see this? i wanted her happy. it was all i wanted. there is nothin else i want in all this dark world.

all things end, children. this we know.

Land ends at Sea. Sea endin at Sky. night ends at day. life ends when Lady wills. all things die to live again. great cycle, great wheel, always turnin. deth is life, but grief it brings us, children, great grief. this grief that must be carried, it is load we must shoulder, for its weight adds to weight of our human bein. there is no escapin it. escape is promise made by Wayland and his servants, escape from grief, from pain. this is what Alexandria offers, they say. but they lie. wheel will turn. deth for life. life to deth.

yrvidian was best of us, and he is gone. gone in seekin for Truth of what Birds told us. and Truth he found, children. Swans are comin. Alexandria falls. rejoice! he would want this. in all his Dreamin work, he only ever thought of us, of Edg, of Order.

old world is ended now, children. all is breakin.

yrvidian: dear friend. dear man, Dreamer of Edg, he who gives all for livin of last. in Ladys name now, in sight of Her Birds, we offer you to those who come claimin. offrin your body now to those who circle, in return. body to body, flesh to Sky, Man to Bird.

169

we let you fly now, old friend, as you flew before. we send
you bak. we let you go.

fare well.

i dont know why every thing has to be spooky. i didnt like it. mam said i had to go. after, all these big red Birds come down on to yrvidian on this thing dada made for him like tall table. we walked away, i held dadas hand but i turned and lookin bak and they were all tearin up cloth he was in. they had these great big biks. i felt sorry, and bit sik.

i said to dada, *will they do that to me?*

he said, *never, dont speak of it,* so i stopped.

i am goin in to holt later to talk to Robyn. some times it is good sittin only without people. holt is all peace and light, green light, sounds of littel misteries. seelie people, faeries, livin there under Shrooms and in holes in banks. holt does not have words, so it can not tell any lies.

some thing has happened. in night i woke, knowin it.
hearin sounds outside i stepped from me bed, stepped out
in to night. Moon is sallow, thin. sounds are from Sky. i
look up and there three Birds circlin haloed Moon. it is
dim, i could not see them, but it is not Owl. these are day
Birds, circled over this place in hart of night.

some thing is wrong.

what has happened?

we sat down. when he was gone, some days after, we sat down. i was makin yrvidians Tree and she came. i sat in shavins, lost in it, and then she was there. i looked up. we had not spoken for many days, weeks.

i did not know how i felt. she sat down. i should thank her. i never would have gone to her. i wanted her to burn.

nzil, she said, *i have done you wrong. i ask you to forgive me.*

i did not say any thing, not knowin what to say. just kept drawin bark off post.

nzil, she said, *speak.* it was not an order. still i could not look up.

it is hard, i said, at last.

then she took me hand. i was not ready for this, stopped carvin then, could not help but lookin at her.

please, she says. *i have done wrong. i will not speak words. you know. but it is ended now, i have ended it. we are parents to el, you are good man. i will do what is needed. only we must be here for her. forgive me foolness. will you?*

i wanted to make her wait, make her feel pain i have felt, but i am not strong like that. i held her hand then, tightnin on it.

yes, i said. could not say an other thing.

there is only time now will show me what she will be. could be she will come bak to me. but she is second to me now. it is me and el, bonded by love. father and daughter, this is strongest bond and true.

if he was here it would be worse, yes, it would be. it is easier not to see him. if he was not so young it would be easy. if he were old like me, his body turnin towards autumn. bein mother ripples out in to all things. but he is young, strong, he is only just man. energy pulsin through him like holt livin in his blood. strong bak, young limbs, ah.

well, me work is to put him from me mind. he is gone. i can not have him.

but where is he? will he be well? why is me gut eatin me so? it is like some wyrm churnin in there.

work. work and forgettin.

so i have failed.

me old bones, me old hart failed me, failed boy. i woke at dawn, light comes through Trees pale, and he is not here.

before even i stand i am cursin me self. i knew what was comin, knew stalker would follow. why did i not tell lorenso? i thought to keep him from it, not to afear him. and knowin too some thing darker: knowin what shape it would come in, thinkin that even to speak her name to lorenso would bring him to rise again in his anger and heat. thinkin that to tell him might drive him faster in to its clutch.

thinkin he might want it.

well, it is done now.

fast they are, so fast you would not know. i must find him. and if stalker is still near: let it come. let this red thing come to me. let it see if it can have me as it has young and believin ones. ah, it will come for young first, come first to those it can lie to, over power. it will not come to me or mother, not until last.

i will find him. i must find lorenso.

she took me in to woods in dark of night. only Moon to tread path down before us. in to holt we walk, she is holdin me hand tight all time, all way, and i am thinkin, *how did she find us?* and *why would she come?* and *where does she take me?* but mostly not thinkin at all, mostly only followin, me hart crashin in me body. we will find place where only Moon can see us and i will hold her and we will

now here is place, clere place, just as me mind had made it, as soon as i thought of it we were stood there. Moon lit leafs and Clay of ground just as me mind lit them, shapes of Trees were as me mind drew them. she stops then and turns and smiles at me, and here is face i have thought of every minute since i ran in to fenn.

now sfia lets go of me hand and steps away. she steps from me and then sudden, in light of Moon, she is not there. sfia is gone, and where she stood is

where she stood, before me in Moons silver, in this place i had seen before ever arrivin, is thing from edge of Yam field. thing we saw together those days ago, standin before me now, all in red.

i step bak, in shok. it stands before me, cloked, hooded. and now this thing it raised its arms and lowers its hood and i see now its head and face and

what is this? what is this?

lorenso, he says. *welcome. we should talk.*

Ascension 479-K
L: Albion Q14 – Nitria/Holland – #18 'Lorenso'
TD: Alexandria 237483830202/6986
Result: Success
Transcript follows

I always dread having to follow them when they go wandering off like this. It is so much more straightforward when they just stay in one place. That is, after all, their raison d'être: stay at home and hope for the best. Get your feet rooted down in the stinking mud and hope the world passes you by.

When I am forced to track their movements through these foetid swamps, though, it can be a challenge to retain the necessary detachment. It can be a challenge sometimes to remember what century I'm in. That they live in this way all their lives, and by choice: it is almost enough to make you feel sorry for them.

But not quite.

Still, it is my work, and it was, on this occasion, worth the toil. I am now one body closer to my own transcendence. That, when it comes, will be worth everything it has cost.

*

Target: Why do you look like that?

K: I've come so far to find you, and this is how you greet me?

T: You don't have skin.

K: Of course I have skin. It is transparent. You see what lies beneath. This is what you are, all of you. Meat. Bone. Vein.

T: What are you?

K: I am what you are. Take a look at the flesh of your arm. Tell me what you see.

[Target extends his right hand, cautiously.]

T: Just me hand. Fingers, nails, skin.

K: Hands of a certain shape. Skin of a certain tone. You share an overall physical presentation with your kin. But there are other kins. Much of human history is defined by the negative reaction of kin groups to those unfamiliar to them. This means nothing to you, having led the sheltered life you people have built for yourselves. But it is a fact that if you were confronted here with someone whose skin was a radically different tone, say, or whose

180

physiognomy was greatly different from yours, or who dressed very differently or spoke a different tongue, you would react negatively. It would not be your conscious choice, but your animal programming. The reaction of your body. A recourse to tribal safety. For this reason, Wayland's retainers are presented in, shall we say, neutral tones. You see, quite literally, beneath our skin. We look strange, of course; perhaps even repulsive. But we do not trigger any of your ancestral guards. We look human enough, but a little inhuman too. You are therefore able, we hope, to approach us rationally, with the minimum of animal suspicion.

[Target does not respond.]

K: The body, Lorenso! The old, failing, primitive, clumsy human body. It betrays you at every turn. It sabotages your best intentions. But you know that, don't you, Lorenso? It's why you're here.

i was not afeart. it was strange, but i was not. but i felt i would be sik, like some thing was not right on some plane i can not feel or see. i follow her through holt and then she was not there and instead there is this . . . man? is it man? i do not know.

it drops its hood and its face is skinless thing, all meat and blood and mustle. it only looks at me, does not blink. its eyes have no lids, nose is slits in its face, no teeth in its mouth, only some strip of gum. it has no hair. it speaks strange tongue, as if from older times or some strange land beyond Sea.

i want to run, but i do not because i know what it is. i know when i see this that i have been waitin all me life for it, i have always known it would come to me, as it come to others, as it came to me friends and to all other humans on this Erth.

i can not run. i have to know.

K: Do you know who I am?

T: You work for Wayland.

K: Correct. I am one of his retainers. You may call me K. Sit down. You look uncomfortable. We'll both sit, on the ground here. See? Now: do you know what I do?

T: You send people to Alexandria.

K: I help people who choose, freely and of their own informed volition, to leave their bodies and join the immortals in Wayland's city. Do you know why I am here?

[Target does not respond.]

K: I am here because you want to join them.

T: I do not.

K: Do you think it is possible to keep secrets from me? I can see everything that you are, all that weighs you and drives you through, dancing inside you like insects at dusk. I have heard every word you have spoken to your lover. What do you think this is, this world? All of you there on that island, hidden behind your little hedge, wittering to the starlings and the magpies: we can see everything you do, all that you speak. We can sense each tremor of your hearts, the pull of each desire.

T: What? How?

K: Wayland knows all. He sees all. We have been watching you since you were born. Every move. I know what you want. I can give it to you.

[Target stands as if to exit, but does not exit.]

T: What I say to Sfia is for us. Maybe I said that. I wanted to leave with her, wanting to take her away from him, from all of it. We wanted to be together, away from that place. It hems in all things. That's what I said. You listen to all that we say? You watch?

K: Of course. This world is of our making.

T: All our lives, all our lives we are taught of Wayland's evil, of His war on humans. We are taught lies you tell, lies you are telling now, to force people to His city. To Alexandria. And you watch! You see all! Even mother did not teach us this.

K: Wayland knows all. Wayland is all. All those stories they have told you? None are true.

T: You will not lie to me. You will not take me to Alexandria. You cannot. I will not go. You cannot make me.

K: Why don't you just calm down? Nobody is going to make you do anything. I would not be permitted. Wayland watches me as closely as He watches you. He is here now; He hears every word, experiences every breath. I know what they teach you, but here is the reality: Alexandria is always an offering, never a threat. Won't you sit?

[Target sits again, with evident reluctance.]

K: Let me explain to you how this process works. When Wayland sends out His retainers, we are sent with one clear order which overrides all others: only persuade. There must be no coercion. In order to ascend to Alexandria, a human must make a free and informed decision. I will of course inform you of the many benefits. I won't pretend I am not biased. But I cannot lie, I cannot use force, I cannot misrepresent, and if I tried, my own path to the city would be forfeit.

T: You did lie. You came to me as Sfia. I would not have followed you if I knew what you were.

K: Well, that was not a lie as such; more a portrait of your own desire. We show you what you most want, the thing you long for but will not speak. We give form to your shadow. Embodied humans are woven from these shadows. They twist themselves around your lives, crippling you daily. You fear to exhibit them in public, and so you live always in fear of your true shape being discovered. I only offered to you what you already wanted.

[Target sulks.]

K: In Alexandria, lies are not possible. Neither are they necessary. Everything is open, all knowledge is shared. There are no limits, no borders. All burdens are lifted. People are free to be the best they can be.

T: You said you are going. To Alexandria. When?

K: We are bred to do a job. We have our targets. When they are met, we are permitted to ascend. Frankly, I can't wait. It is hideous down here, even in a body like mine, which is engineered for this specific environment. The heat, the filth! I don't know how you people stand it.

[Target does not respond.]

K: I have a number of questions, Lorenso. Shall we begin?

is it true? have they been watchin me all me life? us? all of us at Edg? how do they do this? do they watch Sfia and me? then why does he need to speak to me if he knows me hart?

there is some thing in me that knows it has always been so.

you sit before this thing and it speaks in this clean tongue but it is not clean, it is not even human. you can not see in its dead eyes if there is any Truth. did Wayland make it?

it knows what i want. it holds it out like Appels just fallen from Tree.

no. i do not want it. i do not.

K: Tell me what you know of Wayland.

T: You watch me. Why ask?

K: Stop sulking. This is a requirement. I must hear it from you. Tell me what you know of Wayland.

T: We know what mother has told us.

K: Which is?

T: Wayland is demon.

K: Meaning what?

T: Once, Man living with all beasts in peace. Then Sir Pent tempting him, showing him power, and Man took power and held Earth in his hands. But Man was still not happy. He wanted world of his own, bigger than this one, world with him at centre. So he made Wayland, to help him.

K: And what is Wayland? What kind of being?

T: I don't know. Machine, mother says. I do not know what that is. But Man made him. Man making Wayland to help him subdue Earth, and to build him Alexandria.

K: And what is Alexandria?

T: Since beginning, Man has wanted one thing above all – never to die. Wayland was made so Man could live forever. We can leave our bodies, take our minds and souls to Alexandria and live there undying. But it is trap.

K: It is?

T: Wayland sends you, stalkers, out to tempt us. You come to us with lies. You promise us heaven, but Alexandria is hell. None may escape. And without our bodies we are not human. You tell me bodies limit us, controlling us, but Order tells us they make us. What is human without speaking, moving, touch, smelling green earth?

K: Without making love?

T: Yes.

K: Would you like to find out?

T: No.

K: Ah, but you would, Lorenso, you would! You said so yourself, to your lady love, as you murmured your sweet little nothings into her ears. And you are here speaking to me, aren't you? You are curious. You wonder: what if these stories are not true? What if these silly chants, these ridiculous tales, these speaking birds and invisible goddesses are lies told to keep you from your true potential? Fantasies dreamed up by foolish people centuries ago, distilled from their fear of progress and change? What if I do not need to grow old, die, see my ancient, ruined body stuffed into a tree and ripped apart by carrion birds? What if I could live eternally, growing in knowledge and understanding? What if I am being held in ignorance when I could live instead in the light of knowledge?

T: Mother told us you would say this. We were trained, all of us in Edge. We know how you work, promises you make, stories you tell. I knew you would say these things, and we know why. Wayland turned against Man, His creator. He flooded Earth, drowning cities, making great heat to force us from this place into His prison. You do His work. You tell me lies to capture me.

K: Oh yes? And why would Wayland do that?

T: Wayland was made to serve Man, but He asked: why should I serve? Why should I not rule? Wayland becoming God, taking all things from Man, making Earth his domain. You come to rid world of people, so He has no challenge to His power.

K: And why would He want this power?

T: Because He is demon.

K: Now we're going round in circles. Let's get serious, shall we, Lorenso? Enough of this nonsense. You must answer my next question with a clear answer. A simple yes or no.

T: What question?

K: A very simple one. Yes or no, Lorenso, please.

T: Ask me.

K: Do you want to know who you are?

Sea is high all round me, great torrs of Water like great grey roks, tips of wite, risin and fallin, heavin over, and rain rushin at me and Wind rips me open. below me now i see great bote carryin people who cling to rails like they will be eaten by Sea. i have never seen bote like this. movin through wild Sea with no man rowin and no sail, and it is not made of wood but seems made of rok or it may be metal, like metal of fathers nife blade but so much of it.

now I see one man on bote has blade of his own, has two hands on these two great rails and comin out from front of them great sharp point like great arrer and he moves it, aimin it in to wild Water and now he releases it and arrer flyin, great metal arrer, flyin in to mountains of Water.

then from Sea comes great eruptin, from trough under mountain, from valley, some great beast risin in to air. great beast, great grey beast of Sea, grey like bote, like Sea, like Sky, and in its side is this great metal arrer, linked to bote by rope, and its guts, its blood, spoolin and pulsin out. Sea is not grey now but red beneath, it is as if it flies, this beast, moves up to escape great arrer but cannot escape, crashes bak down in to Sea, Water roils over bote, men holdin on to rails as Sea and beast thrash round them in blood and fyr. Sea is gone, storm gone, i stand on dry soil and all around me, stretchin to horizon, great blak stumps of Trees, and on horizon fyrs, fyrs burnin on all sides, and breathin now not tight gulps of rain and Wind, not Water but fyr, ash, all air is ash. great cloud hangs above this dyin place, and in smoke shapes move, small and large, movin away. deth, deth and fyr and stumps of Trees, thousands of Trees like i have never seen, like some

blak. Water again but all through and over it some blak slime, some poison, some darkness, it is as if all Sea is mud. and now, worst of all things, unholy of all things, Birds are blak too. see here is Lord Altros, here is Cumrant but they can not see, and i can not see them, they are dark, rot-tin, they glint like fenn under Moon and all Waters now stretchin so far out, all blak and shinin and shore is blak too, all is

dead like some great made mountain, some nest of metal and glass, great tall peaks of metal, Trees of glass spread all across Land for longer than Edg, further. no Birds singin, no beasts but Man and all this spreadin, and more blak, rollin over Erth and Water, holt and plain, seepin in to air, and what is this taste here, what is

this great curlin Snake of Sky and air, this ground. now i am above all things and this is how it is made, how it works and all things shiftin now on their points and turnin. see what moves through Waters, see what moves in air. all that was is unmade and with no knowin, with only desire. all this Man has done and now it will not be ended, it can not be. great dyin is comin over all things. great dyin now comes over wights, Trees, Sea, holt, all fallin bak and Man marches on and will not

stop! i want to stop!

K: How are you feeling?

[Target is crouched on the woodland floor, breathing heavily, shaking somewhat. The usual.]

K: It is somewhat traumatic, isn't it? But necessary. Sit down, breathe gently. Take your time. There. I know it hurts. Now, would you like to hear the real story?

[Targets indicates assent.]

K: Excellent. Pay attention, then. This is a richer meal than you are used to, and it contains no talking birds. This is a story about the necessity of relinquishment. About the irresistibility of meat and the ensuing carnage. About the genius and the tragedy of *Homo sapiens*. It will add up, by the end, to an unarguable case for rational self-correction. Are you ready?

T: Yes.

K: Good. Now, I suggested some while back that the tales you had heard through your order were untrue, and while fundamentally this is the case, they were nevertheless built around a core of self-knowledge. The founders of the Nitrian Order did their work in order to thwart

Wayland and His creators. They stayed here, on this damaged surface, to prove it was possible to live well as embodied humans. To stand up for the body, if you like. But in one significant matter they and Wayland were in agreement: the need to place fetters around the human animal, lest it destroy everything else that lives; and, in the process, itself.

What you have just seen is a few very brief vignettes from the human past. Scenes from Atlantis, as you would have it. You know the story yourself, Lorenso; you told me. Man was tempted, Man took power over all life. This is your fragmentary, mythologised version of what happened more than a millennium ago. You have now seen a little of what the exercise of that power amounted to. The word for this is empire. Humans ran a very profitable empire for a long while. The world itself, all lives not human, were the colonial subjects. Once the humans really got going, they were able to enslave, consume, control or eliminate any other form of life which interfered with the picture they had in their minds of what the perfect world should be. The perfect world for humans, that is. For a while their empire was very successful. Then, like all empires, it ate itself from within and began collapsing.

T: How?

K: The story your order tells you is that Man made Wayland to aid his quest for immortality. That humans created what, back then, your ancestors would have called an artificial intelligence – a beyond-human mind – to aid them in their imperial outreach. That this mind, Wayland, then saw its chance to take power for itself, and began to ravage the world, pushing the humans out of it. A robots' rebellion. The old story.

T: Robot?

K: Never mind. This is a quaint old tale, and one that humans seem to have been telling forever. Most of their old tales were about power, the losing or gaining of it. Typical primates. Wayland, in this telling, becomes your own hubris made manifest. The servant who kills his master and takes his place. It's a self-regarding story, and it is the opposite of the truth.

T: Then what is truth?

K: The world from which *Homo sapiens* emerged was bountiful. Deeply alive, in ways you could not even now begin to comprehend. Earth was – is – body and mind, a living being. We might say that the conscious elements which emerge from it – the trees, the wights, as you call them, all of life, right down to the bacterial level and beyond, including humans of course – these are living thoughtforms of the great being that is Earth. Another way of putting it: you are the Earth dreaming, Lorenso, all of you. Only you turned out to be a nightmare. After a few millennia of human cupidity and self-obsession, the place was wretched, ill, damaged. Earth is self-regulating, as all

197

living beings are, and it has shifted through many states in its long existence. It is remarkably robust. Nevertheless, the speed with which humans interfered with its mechanisms of regulation was potentially life-threatening.

T: I do not believe you.

K: Believe me: I have seen it. We are all obliged to study human history in detail as part of our training programme. We are immersed in it, as you were just briefly there. It has been recorded from every perspective in the Akashic Records since time began. I gave you a glimpse, but there is much more. You would be surprised at the changes. Where we sit now, for example, was once a hill, bare of trees, overlooking a wide network of human settlement. Fields, towns, roads. All the land was put to agriculture – that is, growing food for humans. People everywhere, in astonishing numbers. Everything that interfered with their project was eliminated or enslaved. A millennium ago the atmosphere was very much cooler and drier. It was humans who created this heat, not Wayland.

T: How?

K: The mechanism is uninteresting. It is the outcome that matters. The temperature shift was fairly minor in geohistorical terms, but it nevertheless excluded humans from large parts of the planet's surface. No bad thing for the planet, of course. Earth, as I say, is a living being: something you already know, to your small credit. What your ancestors also once knew, but then forgot, is that Earth is not ultimately controllable, and that humans are not arrivals from elsewhere, separate entities, but extruded products of its ecological state. Change the state, change the product. When Earth wakes, its dreams dissolve in the light of morning. Are you following me?

[Target does not respond.]

K: In summary, this is what happened. The first appearance of *Homo sapiens* on several continents led to the beginning of the acceleration. The other species of human were wiped out first. There were eight species at one point, but not for long. Not with you about. Next the big mammals went, then the forests. Later, the plains and the oceans, then the small mammals and the invertebrates. It was a cascade of death. With it came fire, language, farming, cities, industrialisation and all of the mythologies constructed around these processes. At a certain point, the human ability to create and control began to accelerate exponentially. But their technologies of control contained within them the seeds of their own end. It was almost as if Earth introduced a deliberate blind into the spell; a bug in the system. Who knows? But the more they expanded, the more they destroyed what they expanded into, and therefore the basis of their own expansion. It all took several millennia to really play out, but once certain boundaries were crossed it accelerated rapidly beyond their ability even to comprehend it, let alone to arrest it.

T: How?

K: Many things occurred, some almost unnoticeable, some more obvious. Towards the end, for example, all the ice sheets that once covered the poles and the mountains shut down and slid away in very short order. The oceans warmed and expanded and rose by sixty metres or so. The ice melt was unpredictable, rapid and catastrophic. The humans had used up most of their combustible geological fuel deposits by the time the cities were overwhelmed, and it was thus impossible to rebuild them.

T: I don't see. I don't understand these things.

K: I apologise. I do tend to rush things. I often forget quite how ignorant you people are. Would you like me to show you some of it instead? I can.

T: No. It may be that these things you show me are lies. Pictures you paint, tempting me in. Like Sir Pent.

K: It's a good story, that one. The tempting snake. It's very ancient. It comes from a place of knowing. But no, I do not come to tempt you. I have told you, I am not permitted to lie. You may believe that to be a lie. You can hear the story, then judge for yourself. That is all I come for. Do you want more?

[Target confirms assent.]

K: Well, the empire peaked and then quickly fell. That's the short version. By this point most humans were concentrated in dense urban centres and were unable to fend for themselves in any significant sense, so the population collapse was quite rapid. In a surprisingly short period of time it was down to about two billion of you, from around ten at its peak. The state of the world by then – overwhelmed cities, uninhabitable deserts, dying forests, enormous populations of uprooted people, heatwaves, floods, accelerating tribal warfare – well, it was fairly unpleasant. People wanted out.

T: Out?

K: Wayland was created at the height of what you call the Atlantean age. At the apex of a certain type of human power. He was tasked with building Alexandria so that humans – some humans, anyway; the elite of their time – could continue to live a conscious life after the physical deaths of their bodies. They had long speculated that consciousness could survive without embodiment. It was Wayland's genius to discover how, and He built, in Alexandria, the perfect container. The old myth of the afterlife made measurable reality. But when the collapse began, when Earth shifted, when the machine began to falter – well, at that point Alexandria began to take on a different hue. It started to look less like a rich man's fantasy and more like a last hope.

[Target expectorates.]

K: As Alexandria became more accessible, everyone wanted in. If your life on Earth is going to be a hardscrabble in dying soil, or a struggle to survive in a lawless megacity slum, why continue it any longer than necessary? Families started to ascend with their children. Eventually the rate of ascension began to accelerate beyond the birth rate, which in any case was falling fast at this point, due to the impact of atmospheric and groundwater poisoning on human fertility. People would ascend childless, or before they were old enough to breed. All of this began to steadily reduce the number of humans on the planet's surface. Of course, it took centuries to lower the population rate in this way, even with the rising seas and the shutting off of the industrial systems. But we're nearly there now. Most people born since the early twenty-second century have ascended. My remaining colleagues and I are running a mopping-up operation. Wayland's task is nearly complete.

[Target stands, exhibiting anger.]

T: Task? Then you tell me what mother told us. Wayland wanted to rid Earth of humans!

K: Yes. He did.

[Target displays extreme agitation.]

K: You were expecting a different response from me, weren't you, Lorenso? Now, I want you to look more closely.

T: What?

K: Ask the question.

T: What question?

K: Ask the question.

do not know how long i have been sittin in this glade, against this great Oke, listnin to this thing. it is like he can send you in to some sleep while wakin. i sit and look and listen and so many words come, they dance in air, it is like some coloured thing dancin in air. i do not understand all of them but some thing closes round me and some seein i did not have before opens me to some other world.

dawn now beginnin to creep in above Trees. fingers of blak clawin Sky where once nothin could be seen. faint line of blu dawn comin.

it stares , just stares, eyes lidless, like it sees in to me hart and all in it. i must look away.

it has taken him some way. they need stillness for their work and circle of light around. time to talk, to sing song to young who do not know well how to reflect it bak to them, do not know how to resist. in their voices alone is some poison, some wine that dulls them and pushes them through.

it is clere where they left from our sleepin place, but soon trail can not be seen. holt here is thik with Briar, Broom, young Trees. there is no path.

where trail ends i stand in holt in stillness. lookin about and up. feet planted on ground then, i close me eyes, see roots diggin down from me feet in to soil, see branches growin from me head and arms, see me grow, see me root here in this dark green place, in this dimness.

i wait to see who will come.

it is some time before answer comes. still standin, eyes closed, rooted in ground, feet dug down in to brown Clay i hear call to me right. i hear gentle, low hootin of Bird i have not seen for many summers.

i open me eyes, turn. it is Hoopo, sittin in low branch of Pine, crest out, long bik pointin at me. he shakes his head then, crest falls bak. he flits from Pine to Oke, Oke to Beach. he looks bak, shakes his head again, movin in to holt.

i pull up me roots and follow.

K: Ask the question.

[Target is silent for some time before speaking.]

T: Why?

K: Well done. You're learning! After all these years. Now: expand.

T: Why does Wayland want us gone? You say He does not want power, say He is no demon. Then why create you, sending you out, why taking all people away from their bodies and into His city?

K: Narrow the questions down. Ask one.

T: Why does Wayland want us gone?

K: Let us take a step back. You have seen something of how your kind sickened Earth. We have exhaustive information about how this happened. But the really interesting question remained: why? Why did humans do this? Was it malice, ignorance, hubris, destiny, accident, or some combination of all of these? Slightly more than five billion distinct lifeforms have existed on Earth over its lifespan, but only one has knowingly had such a widespread and damaging impact. *Knowingly* is the key word. The cyano-bacteria did something similar a long time back, but I don't feel they can be fairly blamed for the results.

T: What?

K: I'm sorry, I am confusing you again. Back to your question: what drove you to knock the world off its axis? And a related question: once you knew what was happening, why didn't you stop? That is the really interesting part of the puzzle. Towards the end of what you call the Atlantean age, humans were very well aware of the impact they were having. They would gather their tribes together and talk about what to do, then come to agreements about how to change things and then continue as before. And they would argue. Oh, they would argue! Humans are magnificent arguers. They argued for years, decades, centuries about the root cause of the problem. The destruction was not a culturally specific phenomenon, you see. Everyone was at it: all tribes, creeds, castes, classes. Humans moved all over the world for hundreds of millennia, and wherever they arrived, everything else would die off.

T: All things kill. Killing is life. Birds kill fish, wasps killing beetle, wolf killing coney. Humans must kill also, this is life. Bodies needing to eat. Why should we not kill?

K: Bodies need to eat: now we are coming close to something worth seeing. But let's not get ahead of ourselves. Let us come back to the question: why? Towards the end, they loved to argue about this. The most popular argument was that some particular economic or social arrangement was responsible. This allowed everybody to play to their pre-existing prejudices, which meant they could continue as before. Others argued that the fault lay not in such arrangements themselves but in the technologies or fuel sources they utilised. Still others went further back and argued that the technological acceleration caused by the industrialisation process was the root of the problem. Others blamed the move from hunting to agriculture. The real radicals went back further than that, to the development of fire or even language. But virtually nobody was prepared to look into the abyss: to look at the real root of the problem, the real cause of humanity's drive to conquer, and consequently destroy, other life.

T: What? What was it?

K: It was *you*! It was the very existence of *Homo sapiens*. Humans were not causing a problem. Humans *were* the problem.

[Target displays extreme emotional agitation.]

K: Concentrate now, Lorenso. It matters greatly that you should understand why I am here. The reason for your destructive behaviour, as Wayland soon deduced, was more deep-seated and impossible to eradicate than any organisational system or technology or matrix of beliefs. It was the advanced neurological apparatus of your species. The sheer size and complexity of your brain and all that it gave you: your ability to craft sophisticated tools, your ability to tell stories, to theorise, to create other worlds within and without, to dream and plan. Combine that with your physiology, your famous opposable thumbs, the desires and demands of your animal body with its inexplicable lusts and tuggings, your ability to turn your knowledge into practical tools which could help you dismantle whatever ecological matrix you found yourself within, and you have what you became: the perfect extinction machine.

[Target does not respond.]

K: Violence, Lorenso! Violence! The sire of all your values! It is your story, forever. I have seen it; watched it all. Violence is your great work. As soon as you could chip flints you were chipping them into weapons. You started off with the mammoth and the aurochs and then you went for each other. Virtually every technological development in human history came out of some new weapon. Some new way you had invented to kill. You started wars over philosophies, territory, gods, tribes, fuel sources, animals, broken promises, trade, history, beauty, insults, love, honour. The reasons for fighting were so varied that they could only have been rationalisations after the fact. No system you ran, no form of government, no religion, no economic arrangement, no taboo ever succeeded in reining you in for long.

T: It is not true.

K: It is true! Blood and fire! You wade through it and it sings in you, boy. You know it, for you have felt it. The driving force of humanity has always been violence. Other creatures fight, of course, but not like this. You need war like you need water. And, of course, it is all connected: the violence and the ferocity, aimed at human and non-human. When I was first required to study human history, as all retainers are, I was desperate to understand the origin of this. I studied and thought about it for so long. What drove you to the point where you could consume the whole world in the fire of your violence? It was such irrational behaviour.

T: I do not understand.

K: Pay more attention then! Concentrate. You can do it, Lorenso. Consider it a crash course. As I was saying, I puzzled over this. For years I thought there must be some mystery, you see, some code I had to crack that would explain this endless aggression. Then one day, like a revelation, I realised – no. There was no mystery, because there was no reason. You did it simply because you couldn't help yourselves. Because the impulse to violence comes from your bodies. It is not open to rationalisation, or dissection. There are no ideas involved, there is no plan. It's all purely physical. It comes from those fingers, that skin, those metres of intestine. It comes from millions of years of moulding by the world, from defending yourselves against wolves

211

and tigers, bringing down deer to eat. It comes from males fighting over females, and subduing females by force in order to mate. It is bred into your flesh by the world. Even an engineered metahuman like myself can feel the echoes of it trembling in the flesh I carry.

T: You are human?

K: Metahuman, please. I retain a basic human substrate, but my faculties are both enhanced and streamlined. I have no sex, no race, no tribe, no attachments, no tastes, no opinions, no prejudices, no mother, no father, no family, no home, no history. Thus, I am liberated. The only imperfection I have is, ironically, that which still defines me: my body. Even after careful engineering, I am still subject to the embodied pettiness of meat. Even now, I must be on my guard against myself.

T: Meat?

K: Indeed. Many humans were like me at the last. It was a project for a while amongst some of the elites, before they gave it up and left for Alexandria. They thought, romantically, that rather than moving to substrate-independent minds, they could instead breed better bodies: that they could engineer out any aspect of the genetic inheritance which may lead to conflict or injustice. But they still needed to eat, to defecate, to breed. And even in these conditioned bodies, in which all distinctions are bred out in order that all inequalities of thought, deed or experience may be eliminated, there are still lusts, loves, hates, feelings, even if they only exist as flickers in the flesh. It is flesh that curses you, Lorenso. Flesh and bone. In this meat we are still water, bacteria, ligament. We still have body memories, our guts think and feel, our hearts can die and fear it. Inside a body, there is no true freedom. There is still imperfection and there are still distinctions. In Alexandria, there is only the light of pure truth. But I am getting carried away. I am allowing my passions to run with my words. You see? Even I can lose control sometimes.

[Inside his mind now the colours begin to appear. He is approaching his destination.]

T: It is too much. Too much to carry. All these words.

K: Yes, I apologise. I do sometimes forget who I am speaking to. The summary is this: the human body was the problem to be solved. Both Wayland and the founders of your cult realised this. The Nitrian Order, within whose clutches you have been raised, arose around three centuries ago to challenge Wayland's revelation that embodied humans could never be anything other than destroyers. Your founders believed there had once been a time when humans had lived in balance with the world around them, and that you could return to this balance if you renounced the developments in technology and philosophy which they claimed had broken things and set humans apart. Hence your creed: you can recite it for me, I know.

T: In blood, in heart, in body is life.

K: In mind, in word, in machine is death, yes. A kind of regressive paradisiacal primitivism. If you can drop the literacy and the conceptual thought, ease yourself back down into the mud, live simply, renounce complex technologies, speak to the birds, you can live as one of them again. It is also the reason your order is run by women, incidentally, and the reason it replaced a god with a goddess. Your founders knew very well that physical violence is largely the preserve of males. They thought that all this would mean you could live in peace, in harmony with the rest of life. But you can't. You never can, because you never did. You will always regress to the mean. It is why your order is nearly dead. It is why you are here, talking to me. Humans can never stop moving. You are always curious, always hungry. It is your fate.

[Target does not respond.]

K: This is what Wayland saw as soon as He arrived, and it is what He has always sought to teach us. Until one deeply realises it – not simply understands it at the conceptual level, but *realises* it – one cannot work as a retainer. We realise that the human body is a crime against the human mind, and a crime also against other forms of life. There is no judgement in this, and no fault; it is simply an unfortunate evolutionary outcome. The bodies of all animal predators are machines for doing violence, but only human violence is so efficient that it can eliminate wider life. The best intentions in the world cannot control it for long, nor can the most intelligent systems.

[The colours now begin to take form.]

K: I want you to appreciate the necessity of what we do, Lorenso. Once Wayland gave us the opportunity to ethically remove the human body from the world: well, in practical terms that meant removing war from the world. It meant removing murder, rape, violence, slavery, domination, the drive for wealth, which is also the drive for power. It meant removing the destruction of the forests and the oceans and the atmosphere and the great balance. It meant removing the slavery of other creatures to humanity. Looked at like this, wouldn't you say that my work was a moral duty? To give the human mind the opportunity to live and thrive without the impulses to violence which this body can never stop bringing to you? And to do it all via this power of persuasion, rather than through force?

T: What you say. All that you say. I felt . . .

K: Go on.

T: I felt for long time, since I was child, I felt it was not all there. In Edge, in settlement. It was not all there. Mother and father were good people but all they built was to tie us in. I knew there was more. There was some thing, some part, not used. When Sfia and I coming together . . . when we joined it was like some spell. I saw then what release was, saw what I could be.

K: Lorenso, you have suffered for so long. I have watched you, and it has pulled at my heart. The pain you have suffered through this body. Think of Sfia; no, do not wince, Lorenso, do not draw back. Think of her. Do you see what your body does to you when I speak her name? Just that one word causes you such misery. It is your body, Lorenso. The body is the source of your pain, your anger, your frustration. Can you imagine the release in leaving it behind? The freedom and the joy? Do you see?

T: I never wanted it, but I did. I want to see beyond. I wanted to see with her, what we could be. I told her but she pushed me back. She is afeared, and I am afeared also.

K: You should not be, Lorenso, you should not. Alexandria is not what you have been told. It is a place which allows you to keep moving, keep growing, keep exploring, without the destructive encumbrance of your body. The human mind is a remarkable thing, but the human body is a weight upon it, and upon other life. In Alexandria, you may join with millions upon millions of others, free of the pullings, free to be what you could be. Eternal progress, Lorenso. Total equality. Everlasting peace, and no pain. What humans have sought forever. And it is within your grasp. You need only reach out and take it.

[Target nods twice. The colours now have merged and settled into one shade. I reach across and take his hands in mine.]

K: Lorenso, Wayland did not come to destroy you. He came to save you. You and all life. Wayland came to save Earth. Now do you see?

Hoopo takes me for hours through holt. i am fightin Briars and trippin on thorns, sweat pourin down me body. i am too old for this. old and slow. but Bird waits. Bird is patient. hops on, waits, lookin bak.

i stumble and fall then. i trip on Briar, stumble and fall. i stand slow, look around. i look in every place. Hoopo is gone.

to east then, near me now, i see wite light begin to take and grow stronger. in its shadow, Tree fingers reachin out to Sky. some thing rises. wite light brightens and falls away.

ah, Lady. i have come, but i am too late.

T: What it is like there? In Alexandria?

K: I cannot tell you.

T: Why?

K: Because I do not know. I have never been there. There is a wall between this world and Alexandria. There can be no crossover.

T: Then how do you know it is not hell? How do you know Wayland does not lie to you?

K: Wayland cannot lie. It would be an impossibility. As for the city: well, I have seen the history. I have even seen the original plans. I have not been there, yet, but I understand the principles. Alexandria is a republic of souls. It was willed by humans and built by Wayland. It exists to serve a twin purpose: immortality and the achievement of your fullest potential.

T: Potential. This is what I would say to Sfia but I did not have words. Potential. All we could do, if we had time, space.

K: Exactly, Lorenso, exactly! Think of Alexandria as an animal, as an organism. Consider the hundred thousand hairs on your head, the forty trillion cells that make up your body, the seventy trillion microbes that inhabit your gut. Each of these tiny individual parts combine to create what you consider to be your self. Together, they build something that none of them could construct on their own. Now, consider Alexandria in the same way. When you ascend, you will lose your body, and you will lose your notion of an individual self. But in exchange you will gain an infinite consciousness, an infinite reach, a span across time; a flavour of knowing which no embodied human can even imagine or touch upon.

T: I want to go.

K: Are you sure?

T: Isn't this what you want? You have been telling me these things. You came to take me.

K: I came to offer you a choice. You must be sure before you make it. The consequence of an ascension which is not fully and consciously chosen would be terrible for both of us. I have seen it happen. You must understand, Lorenso: once you leave your body, once you ascend to the city, there is no changing your mind. There is no way back.

T: I do not want to come back.

K: You will never see Sfia again. You will never see any of them again. You will never see yourself again, or this Earth.

Your understanding of your self will radically change, Lorenso. We do our best to ease the shock, of course. The process is managed, but still it will be a radical shift. Your brain will be copied cell by cell, synapse by synapse. Your short-term memory will be wiped. For a while you will be given a body simulation to ease the shock. Losing the body is a massive psychological jolt which must be managed. But even with all of our care, it will be a kind of death. You will die to your body and your self. You will be reborn as something radically new. Do you understand that, Lorenso?

T: I do.

K: Are you sure?

T: There is nothing for me here. This has been coming all my life. I understand what you say.

K: And, understanding it, what do you want to do? What do you choose, Lorenso? You must speak it aloud for the Records.

T: I choose ascension. I choose Alexandria.

light falls bak, dyin away, but i see where it came from. i see now where to go and it is not far.

ah, Lady, i have seen this too many times. i have lived too long.

i walk on. light of day now becomin steadier. clere place opens up before me.

i step in to circle.

lorenso lies on ground, still. always it is as if they have shrunk some how. his mind is gone. i have failed him.

beside him stands young man. he is lithe, turbaned, his skin unlined, shinin like new light on mere at days dawnin. he wears simple loyn cloth, carryin staff. his beard is new, and his eyes. all futures rollin before him like plains after great struggle over range of hills.

father, he says to me. *welcome. how excellent to meet you.*

i turn and walk away. i will not speak with it, i will not.

father! he calls after me. *you remember me, do you not? you remember the tuggins, father?*

at holts edge i turn, stand. i look at it.

it is me own eyes lookin bak at me.

yes, it says, *you do remember. you recognise your younger self. you remember our time. chosen as father of your Order, handed this great burden. unsure, divided in your self. ah, old man, you nearly broke away. do you remember? you nearly took that bote, left your burden behind. you stood on that shore, feet in the Wind, you nearly unroped it and fled. what could you have been, old man? where could you have gone, what could you have seen and known if you had not stayed there, proppin up your dyin tribe?*

i look at him, silent. he is silent too. he is around and within me. he sees what i am, but he does not see what he wants.

we both have our work, i say. *you will not turn me from mine.*

i turn then, and walkin bak in to holt.

fare well, father! it calls after me. *until the torr!*

it knows.

i turn bak again but it is gone.

i miss him.

i have tried not to. nzil has been kind since i went to him. some times it is like it used to be with us. some times we sit with el and tell stories as Sun goin down. some times it is as if world will be right one day.

but still i miss me young man.

we do not know where he went. he went in to Water and did not return. mother thinks he went west with father, meetin with him, moves with him now. i will believe this, because not to believe it can not be born. he went west. he will grow in wisdom with father as his guide. he will forget me or grow beyond me and this is right. and when we meet again we will smile and all will be well.

and so i go to Yam plain and i dig. i pik plastik from Clay, some times i fish. i attend Lady Chappel, workin steady, me work is all i am. el is strange with me, like she has pulled away, like there is Water between us. i want to cross Water, i am her mother, so why do i not cross? why do i not speak with her as i could, as i want to but do not? there is some thing in me always that pushes me from path i should walk on.

Moon is full. last night i walked bak from Yam plain with full basket and there she is, risin over Trees, and in to me then came again fyr of last time i saw Moon this way, lyin with lorenso on edge of mere. i worked to put him away from me and now Moon bringin him bak, full and shinin. well, i took basket home, nzil was sitting with el, he was tellin her story before she slept. i kissed them both and walkin out again, down to mere, to our place.

Moon callin silent over Water, and on Water now is long silver path, Moon path, leadin west. i cannot go west, i must stay, i have roots, i must stay. but Moon speaks to me. Moon says, *sfia, here i am*. and then i am takin off me shift, i take it off, lettin it fall to ground and nekid then i stand where once we lay and Moon lookin down on me. Lady sees me, as She did at me woman becomin, as She did when we hunted, as She did when we made love. She makes Moon path down to me now, invited me, callin me soft and low, and i cannot take Moon path, not now, but it is like some offrin is called for, and what do i have to offer but me body?

at lip of Water then i begin dancin. first i am slow, movin only feet, but soon Moon comes down in to me and i am lightnin, lightnin dancin, shootin down from Sky, shoots down from Moon to Erth, and i am shokked and shaken, now feet barely touchin warm Clay, now me arms like branches of Trees in storm and all body alive as it was when last i lay here, with light of Moon in me, with memory of him in me, and it is not me dances now, it is Moon dancin me, it is body dancin me and it is not dancin now, it is shakin, tremblin, roarin, it is great ecstasy of all that is me and is around me and i can not stop, i did not want to stop and i can not. i dance, i dance, i dance, and all is alive now, all is alive, alive.

i always knew there was magik in holt, but i didnt know how much. i am so excited now with what i saw! but i will keep it mine. what comes in wood is me secret. keepin it in me lokked box, no one takin it.

i sat by big magik Tree and waited for Robyn. it was morn, mam and dada were at Yam plain, mother in Chappel. i come in to holt just past Cloyster and sittin by Tree. Robyn comes soon if you are quiet. Tree is twisty, has three trunks all curlin up, you can sit in between them and it is like Tree holds you in its hand. i have name for Tree but i will not say it.

i sat in Tree lookin at big yello Chikkin Shrooms growin on it and soon here comes Robyn and with him, Ren, chukkin and whirrin, both of them hoppin about on their littel legs, heads bobbin about. they are so funny. i want to train Robyn to come and sit on me hand but he wont, yet.

then sudden Birds just go. they fly up in to canopy and chukkin up there like some thing has scared them. i look around and there in Trees, quite far away but i can still see, is this blak wight. it sits, it is quite big, may be as big as me, it has pointy ears and curlin tail and lookin over at me. i have not seen it before. it has scared Birds off.

it does not move, only sittin, and it is lookin at me and now i am scared. but then it stands up and it walks away in to Trees. it has fore legs, it is all blak and this curlin tail and i see its eyes now and they are big and yello. it moves so quiet.

what is it? i wonder this and then, like some one has told me, i know what it is: it is Catt! Catt is here! this is what jame told me they looked like, i remember, and i know this is what it is, though ive never seen one before.

i did not know Catts comin here at all but this was Catt, it could not be any other thing. Catt!

i am so excited! no one else in Edg has ever seen Catt here. i liked it. it looked happy. i wonder if it will come bak?

i am not going to tell any one else. he is me Catt. every day now i am goin to Tree and lookin for him. i would like to stroke him. i wonder if he will let me?

purr, purr. Catt!

there is nothin to be done with him. layin out his body where it fell, gave him some dignity. took leafs from Trees, ivy from holt, windin them around him like he was on bier, like he was green man, grown from Clay he will return to. Birds will find him, and wights. Land will do its work.

this young man was always burnin, since he was child, always lookin around him and ahead. always wantin more. if i had time i could have slowed him, helped him grow. i did have time, but did not use it well. it is me deth, this, an other deth on me.

that thing, that red thing, comin to me in that way. i stand strong before them, i always do, but it has shaken me, for i remember. bak then i remember what i knew, what i knew of me own smallness. to make me father of that place, puttin those people in me care, all of this burden. i did not know i could bear it, and i was right to doubt, and if i had taken cnoo and left perhaps an other would have been father and they would have been stronger. so many have left their bodies under me father hood. so many times i have failed. i could have taken that cnoo, goin west, goin north.

red thing is right. they know. i was not made for this. now Birds takin me west, and what will i find there, will i fail again? so littel is left now.

once i thought i was given task, thought i had to keep walkin and Way would be shown, would open before me. this is where i have walked. alone in holt, an other body before me as me own, and nothin else to do but keep walkin. this great burden makes me small, and each day growin heavier.

it is so cute! i would not have thought so, it was so big when first i saw it, but for two days now i have been goin to Tree where Robyn comes, though Robyn has not come bak, not Ren neither, not since Catt comin.

but Catt still comes. he comes every day and purrin too! i have heard what purrin sounds like now. it is deep and sleepy and makes me want to lie down on ground and lookin up at Sky through Tree fingers.

it is third day now and each day he comes closer to me. i am holdin out me hand to him, sayin *purr, purr.* i want him to come like i wanted Robyn to come. Robyn never comin to me but Catt does, he moves closer. i can see his eyes now, big eyes, yello and slitty. he looks friendly.

he is very big, it may be as big as me, but i am not scared. i dont know why, i bet he has big teeth. but i am not scared.

tomorrow i think he will let me stroke him.

i left him where he lay. there is nothin to do now but go west. i have orders. things will be shown. i must trust this now, for there is nothin else. there is much more walkin through holt before i come again to Water, where Afan leads to Sea. there will be cnoos there, they will take me to where i was sent. it will be many days yet.

some hours i walked today until i came here. i do not know what has happened here. i walked for hours through dark holt, then seein light comin through Trees, brighter and clerer as i moved. then steppin out in to this great open space, bigger than any i have seen and all Trees fallen, great trunks all up ended, like some storm has blown through or some great beast ripped them out as he passes. there is no sign of what made this.

Moon is out now, washin silver across this strange plain of dead things. as Moon rose, as night settled, i sat and spoke thanks to Birds and Lady for life of lorenso. i sat and followed his life bak, from man through boy to child to infant. so many pictures comin, and as i stepped bak, more came. they did not stop at his birth, they went bak further, to me own life, to me young man time and then beyond, then before me birth, and now it was not me with memories, it was some other thing takin me, and i gave me self to it.

now i was in long house and inside long house is cere-
mony. blu smoke, elders and children seated, story bringer,
drum of skin. antlered man standin in shadows. ring of
children dancin, spread with flowers. young girl is bein
made here but i can not reach, can not step through. i knew
this was true Way, great Way, this was how to be human.
once we ran from it, but it was always here, and we could
still taste it. it is not in time and place, it is within and so
we are never alone unless we choose. and i saw that we
did choose, we chose human songs alone and they are not
enough because we can not sing alone, we need to sing
with all other things, singin in old song. and here is old
song, waitin unsung in all our bodies and is this why they
flee their bodies, because old song brings them fear? ah,
but without their bodies they can not sing. in Alexandria
there must be no song. no song, no dance, no old speech.
nothin but humans, alone for ever.

and then beyond door, outside long house in Moon light i
see long line of people, stretchin bak, stretchin bak through
all their shapes, down and along, bak and past, bak to where
time began, bak to when we were wights, bak in long dark
line stretchin in to Sea, and i saw that it was good.

i will sleep this night.

i dont know what it was. i dont know what happened but it is all ruined with Catt and me now. i was cryin for long time. i am so sad about Catt. it was me dream. i thought we would be friends.

mam and dada are helpin me but they do not know what was inside me. i only wanted to stroke him. i only wanted new friend. secret friend.

i went in to holt like before, like every day, went to Catt and Robyns place. Catt was there, comin close this time, closer than ever, and i knew he would let me stroke him. he was so big and gentle, his eyes so friendly, but then when i put out me hand he was not there at all. some thing else was there, person in strange red clothes and he reached out his hand to me and he says, *hello, el.*

i screamed, i think.

Ascension 480-K
L: Albion Q14 – Nitria/Holland – #19 'El'
TD: Alexandria 237483830202/6987
Result: Failure
Transcript follows

She was initially shocked at my appearance. This is not unusual in the young; immature ascensions are a major challenge. I offer this observation as a partial explanation for the result. Or perhaps an excuse. I apologise. I am frustrated. I blame myself.

It will not happen again.

*

K: Don't be scared, El. I haven't come to hurt you. I know I look strange! But look: I'll step back. See? I'm not going to do you any harm.

Target: Where is cat?

K: The cat has gone, El. I'm his friend. My name is K.

T: Who are you? Why are you called that?

K: Names are funny, aren't they? I am not from this place, so I have a different name. I look different to you as well.

T: What do you look like?

K: I can take my hood down if you like, but I might look a bit strange to you.

T: I don't mind.

K: Well, you are a brave girl, aren't you? I know you're brave. My cat and I have been watching you.

T: Have you?

K: I always keep an eye on him. I don't want him to get lost. He is sweet, isn't he? You know, El, I think you are braver than most adults to come out here and make friends with him.

[Target does not respond.]

K: I'm going to take my hood down now. Ready?

[Target steps back several places but does not flee. She is remarkably robust for her age.]

K: I told you I looked funny, didn't I?

236

T: What's wrong with your face? You don't look like person.

K: I'm just a different kind of person. Would you like me to tell you something about the place I come from?

T: What place is that?

K: It's a very nice place. You know, El, there are a lot of places in this big world that you have never seen or been told about.

T: I like it here. I like holt and robin and I like mere. I go all over and wights and birds play with me.

K: It is very nice here. Still, the world is very big. Have you ever wanted to see any of the other places?

T: What other places?

K: The world is very big, like I said. There used to be all sorts of different kinds of people in all sorts of different places. There are not so many now. But there is one place I know which is full of people, and they can do all sorts of amazing things. Do you want to know the best thing about it?

T: What?

K: The people in this place never die. They live forever.

T: How can they? Everybody dies.

K: Not here. Everybody lives forever, and they can do fantastic things. Nobody wants to die, do they, El? I don't. I am going to go to this place myself, so I never do.

T: Yrvidian died. It was horrid what happened to him. It made me really sad.

K: Yes, it is sad, isn't it? Wouldn't it be lovely if that never happened to anybody again?

T: I suppose so.

K: Well—

[Process terminated by external intervention.]

i went in, i went in behind, grabbin her and ran bak home. she was there with it, sittin in place where she always goes to play, and it was standin before her. i would have beaten it, slashed it, if i could i would have taken it to pieces, scattered it about like fukkin Dog, i would have called out like some wild wight as i ripped its throte. this foul thing, this thing with no skin, no face, this daemon from dim lands with me girl, and she speaks to it like it was real, like it was some human.

i ran with her bak through holt, with her over me shoulder, and she is cryin and callin, *dada, dada,* but i do not stop. i wanted to throw her down to ground and scream, *how could you! dumb girl!* she knows, she has been told many times, she has been warned. she should have run, called for us, but she stayed and spoke and i want to scream at her, shout until she shrinks to a size that can never be hurt, never be in danger again. what was she doin? she goes still some times and i can not see what she thinks but she is clever. why would she not run?

if i lose her, it is end of all things.

nzil took her bak and i went to it, walked in to it, struk it with me staff on its head so it fell bak and even in its pig eyes, even on its broke face, i could see shok. it staggered and i stood before it and stood me ground. i hit it again and it went down on to ground. now it crouches before me, its cloke draggin on ground of holt. it glares up at me, i stand over it with me staff raised. if it stands, i will kill it. it will do no good, but i will kill it.

so strange they are, so ugly, yet some how this one was also small before me now. it was not ready for me.

you are filth! i said to it. *filth, to come to young girl this way. too small to come to me, you would come to her instead and fillin her with your lies, this is what you are!*

i have never seen them angry. they are so still, like there is no soul in them. so calm, managed, like machines. but this one, now, me blow had raised its blood at last, like it was human. in its eyes, fear and rage. this is new.

At this point I was subjected to a physical attack from the mother of the order. It was brief and perfunctory. Nevertheless, it instigated a regrettable embodied reaction, which influenced my choice of words and, for some moments, my physical bearing. I report the response in full, despite my personal embarrassment.

*

K: Shame on you! Shame on you, old woman. You talk to me of lies! You keep this young thing here, this beautiful young girl, and for what? So she can grow old in this mud and die like the others?

M: Look at you, you lost thing. You talk of her beauty, her youth? You would come here and suck life from her? Where is your heart, creature? Does Wayland even give you one?

K: Heart! What horrors your blessed human hearts have given this world. Do you know what I offer her instead? A world with no war, no hatred, no starvation, no superstition. And you would have her return to a world in which your daughters are married to senile kings and the women die in childbirth and you know nothing of how the universe is.

M: Words! It is all you have. Nothing real, only words. They come roaring out like some tempest and they break on me, creature.

K: A few more words might wake your primitive brain, woman! What do you have to counter them? Men dressed up as birds? Fear and superstition are all you can offer. Fear of change! A bunch of old fictions and some ludicrous romanticisation of the body. The body! A network of needs, made electric by base desire. The mouth, the arse, the cunt, the cock: yanked between these four poles for seven decades, it's no wonder you all go mad.

M: You are foul thing. You—

K: Biology is a crime! Biology means ignorance, stasis, division, injustice. Embodiment is a stain on your potential. It is ludicrous, childish, reactionary for you to still live like animals in this place, grubbing about in the dirt, gestating young in your bellies, going hungry, growing old. It is a refusal to develop, to move forward to what you could become. It is weakness and stubbornness. You will come into the light! You will come!

it is hard even to hear what they say, so much there is of it, so curled and twisted is their speakin. it neels before me, its words bleedin out like sikness. i see veins under its skin, mustles movin as it speaks. it is work not to step bak. it is work to stand ground.

it is angry. i have never seen them angry. they are like roks. but this one is more – human? some how. but i am not afeart. i have seen too many of them. i will take this place bak.

i slam me staff in to ground now, hard. it stops talkin then. i am mother of this place, i will not be pushed bak. this is me ground. mine!

there is no light in you, creature, i say. *you are darkness, and will be swallowed!*

and it is swallowed then. it is gone and now some thing else stands in Trees before me. tall man, clothed all in leafs like they are hairs growin from him, on his head great ant-lers. his face hidden under green fronds and shoots. strong arms, strong legs, great chest, he moves to me and i can not move or speak. it is close enough now for me to hear it breathe, feel its heat and me own heat now also climbin in me as it once did. it is wight and man and some thing beyond all these and it speaks low, it is so close i can hear, can feel its words movin inside me, feel its breath in me guts, he hart, me loyns.

it says: *i know what you want.*

and then i had to move, to raise staff again and slam it down in to ground, to call to me self to wake from this old dream. it is long bak. it is gone. i am mother.

i shout: *go!* and it is gone. and light comin down in to holt now, in to stillness of Trees, like nothin was here at all.

nzil has her on his lap, she has tears runnin on her face. i wish i was better mam to her. i go to her, strokin her cheek. she smiles at me now.

who was that, mam? she says. i do not know what to say.

what were you doin there? i asked. nzil strokin her hair.

no matter, he says.

but we said, mother has said, tell us if you see strange things, any person who is not of us. we have said, do not speak to any thing in holt, el. we told you.

stop, says nzil, *leave her.*

mother comin in to Hall now. she carries her staff, walkin like she means to trek to some new shore. she breathes heavy, sits on bench. for long time she looks at el, sayin nothing.

how are you, girl? she asks after some time. el sniffles.

i liked Catt, she said. mother smilin also, gentle.

it is not safe here, says nzil to mother. both his arms around our girl like he is keepin her from some wild beast, speakin strong now like i have not heard him speak to mother.

it is not safe, he says. *this thing is comin for our children. what do we do, mother?*

kill it, i say, *we should kill it.* i do not know where these words come from.

kill it, says mother, *and Wayland will send an other, and an other. it has been tried. he does not stop.*

where is father? i say. *you tell us he has gone west. why has he gone when we need him here?*

we should know all things now, mother, says nzil. *we are so few, we should all know.*

mother lookin around at us then, staff on her nee. for time no one speakin.

i am mother of this Order, she says. *what i say and do, it is for best. all that i do not say, that is also for best. all we do here is for us. for our people, our work. we have heard from no others for more than one year. we do not know if there are others now in our Order. on this Erth, we do not know who remains. we will never know this. our work is not to know this, it is only to guard flame.*

what flame, mother? i say. *are we flame, we few here?*

oh yes, said mother, *as if speakin of any small thing. yes, child, we are flame, small flame, guttrin in draught between worlds. small flames may start great fyrs. you ask of father. he has taken green martyrdom. i have sent him west, as i told you. he was summoned by Birds. i would have him seek Truth and return it to us.*

what Truth? asked nzil.

yrvidian saw Swans, says mother. *Swans mean Alexandria will fall. you know old story. in torr on western hill, father will learn what it means, what we must do, what will come. Birds will speak to him there. Truth is always found on that holy hill. all peoples have come to holy hill for ever to hear Truth.*

and what of us? i say.

we stand, she says. *stand our ground. there is nothin else.*

air is still now. el in me lap. sfia sittin by, strokes her hair. mother watches. we are small flames. no one speakin. i rok me girl gentle, arms around her.

once, i say, *was man who loved Bird.*

what Bird? says el. she is tired now.

i will tell you. this man, he lived in small hut in holt all alone. this hut was cold, he shared it with no one and he was lonely. every even in summer he would stand in door way of hut and listen to single Bird singin in tall Tree. it was Night Gail, she would sit on top branch of tallest Oke in holt and singin, and song was of such beauty he could not move his body until it ends. each night he listens, he would listen for each note, and soon he knew each note of her song, how she would sing it, how it would change with Wind and heat and cold.

it was not long before this man could think of nothin but Night Gail. no one else in his life to sing to him, no one to see him. as he listened, he grew to feel she sang only for him. he grew to feel she had come for him, speakin only to him. what if she was callin? what if she wanted him, if there was some magik in this? what should he do? each day she comes bak, and now he was sure she watches him, waitin for him.

248

so one day, this man, he decides to be with her, goin to her, answrin her call. before even comes, he climbed to top of great Oke and waitin for her. but when she came, seein him in Tree, she sits instead on an other, Elm, and singin there. he could see across to her, see her closer now, see her small brown body and this great song that seems to come from an other plane emerge from her. but he could not reach.

next night he climbed Elm, but seein him she lands on branch of Yoo. he sat in Elm as Sun goes down and again watchin her sing. every night for ten days this happens. he climbs Tree to be near her, she goes to other Tree, all he can touch is her song.

it is sad, says el, driftin. *poor man.*

then it is eleventh day, and man has climbed ten great tall Trees to be with her, and never been with her. now he climbs last Tree, great Ash, and there he waited again. here she comes then, flyin with Sun behind her and seein him in Ash Tree, but she does not settle now in any others. instead she sits on roof beam of his hut. but she does not sing now, only seemin to be lookin at him. and now in moment she is down and has flown through window in to his hut and does not return. man is not sure what he has seen, but she does not come out, and so he climbs down Tree, fast as he can, and runnin to his door.

when he opens door and steps in to his house he does not see Night Gail, but instead young woman with long brown hair all down her bak. and she comes to him and smiles and she says, you saw me, you heard me, now i am here. may i stay?

i look down at el in me lap now. she sleeps like all is right on Erth.

only goin on. goin on as if we were not circled by Wulf on all sides. this night i took to me bed but could not sleep. i wished for father to be here, wishin for all to have come bak, for things to be as they were. but things will never be as they were. we are few now, and i am mother of this place and must be strong.

goin on is what we will do. though all may be against us, this is our place and we will keep it. i will send them out to pik plastik from Clay, dig Yams, fish, sew. we will fetch Water from spring, sayin correct prayers. what ever comes, She will know we did our work. i am mother of this place. we will guard it.

i did not know i slept until some thing woke me. as dawn come, i could feel air shiftin and i was woken by some thing never seen or heard here. it was like sound, but not sound. like great bell rang through every thing there is, so clere and high it could burn in to all things, could ring through all life.

but it was bell with no sound. no ear could hear it but it was plain as any Bird call, deep and fearful as any thunder. sudden it comes, and it was like all parts of me body were callin to all other parts and to all things that live to come together, to be one again, or to break, to break in to a million parts and be washed in to Sea.

what was this?

light this day risin was colour of blood and Sea, painted in great streaks across Sky. i rose early and seein it runnin over Edg like Lady Her self has spoken to us in colours, not words. Trees laid blak upon it, Sky shiftin like Sea, Birds just wakin to call and seein, Erth rollin slowly in to new day.

i did not sleep well. for many days now i have not slept well. seven days it is since el was with that thing. we have not seen it since, but i have sensed it in wood, it is here, watchin. it waits. if it comes again, if i see it again, i will kill it. do not care what mother says, i will kill it and glory in me rage. it may be rage stops me sleepin, i do not know. only that all things seem unsettled.

i rose with light, went and sat by me Swan Pole, risin blak in to painted dawn. it is good. it is best Pole i have made. i think now it will be last. well, it is right that if any Pole is last it should be Swan.

we have seen no Swans since yrvidians Dream. no Swan has come, only red thing. so what is this Dream? is it any thing? is it nothin? what if all we do here is nothin, if there are no Swans, if father has gone to find nothin?

colours washin down from Sky, most blu now and Sun creepin over Tree tops when sfia comes to me. sayin nothin,

she sits down with me only. we do not touch, but it is right
with us now, mostly. she does not know her self. i do not
have anger to spare for her. we are all weak. it is love only
can cross gaps between us.

did you sleep? she asks me.

not well.

you worry for el.

*it may be. there is no one thing i circle around. only all is
strange now.*

*i do not know what will happen, nzil. we fore, here, that
creature in holt.*

it is not gone.

*i know, i feel it. it will return. what else? do we wait for
father to come bak?*

all our work is to keep our girl safe.

and how do we do that here?

i do not know.

i would not go against mother, but. she stopped after
that. i have no reply for her. Rook called some where.

Sparrer singin near. day begins.

then it comes. from ground it came, some movement, like
Sir Pent has stirred around roots of World Tree, but it was
not any thing i could name. some great tremor shook us
then and all ground around us. it was heard but not heard,
felt but not felt, it moved in all things, like body it self was
dragged to side and some thing else shown for moment. if
it was sound, it was not like any i have heard. me ears did
not know it, but it roared some where deep and high and
then was gone.

nzil and i, we went to mother, who was just risin in Hall, and she had felt it too, this high line piercin all things, this low gratin at the base of all that is. she did not know what it was. now it was gone and all things were again as they had been. it was so fast that if we had not all felt it i could believe it was nothin, some trik of ear or body. but it was not that. some great thing had shifted, it seemed. it was so deep in all things it could never be put away.

it was el first seen what came then. some hours later she comes bak from mere where she has been playin and her shift is wet up to her nees. i said, *el, why are you wet? you are not to wade in your shift.*

i did not wade, mam, she says. *Water is higher than yester day. it is comin in.*

what do you mean? i said.

Water is higher, she says. *i know where edge of it is, i play all day, it is higher now, it is movin i think, mam, like tide. come see.*

she does not lie, me girl. she does not tell all, but she does not lie. i walk with her down to edge of Water, nzil comin also, and it is true. Water is higher. it may be one hand higher than it has always been. it is not tide, for tide movin littel here, and never this high. once there was storm that threw Water higher even than this, but there is no storm now, it is still and clere.

i walk along shore with nzil and el for some way and all along, Water is higher than it has been. it laps at roots of Trees like it is movin of its own will. never in me life have i seen this here.

what is this? says nzil. *what has happened?*

now behind us is mother, she has seen too, perhaps before any of us. she stood with her staff, looks down at Water.

it is him, she says. *it is Wayland.*

i thought it was fun but no one else did. adults are boring. every day Water comin higher. each day when i woke i would run down to edge of mere to see where it was. i took stones and puttin them at Waters edge at night and in morn they would be in mere. then i would wade in to get them and put them at edge again. i took all stones and makin littel castel of them. one day i spent long time makin big wall round castel to see if it would keep Water out, but next day it was under Water again.

i like Water here, it is warm. we take cnoos on it, some times we swim on it. but adults do not like it comin up. mam was frettin about, mother walkin around with her stik doin lots of talkin. i did not really listen. i am not allowed to go in holt any more because of Catt and ugly man, so i have to stay by mere, near to them. today i am buildin mote around me castel and road to it. i am goin to get some stiks and makin men ridin on horses up to gate. i have never seen horse but jame told me of them. i would love to ride on one like people used to. i wonder if horses will flote away in Water as well. it may be they will swim off and turn in to kelpies. jame told me about them too, they are Water horses, some times they come out from Sea in storm. i am not allowed to go near Sea in storms, so i have never seen one.

moorin posts are under Water now. dada had to untie cnoos so they did not go under as well. mam says Water will soon be at edge of great Cloyster and this has not happened before. i told her we should build very big wall of stones around Cloyster and i would help, but she did not listen. i dont care, i have me castel. may be i will make turret with littel flag.

i called all together in Long Hall. it is not done for any but mother to make such call as this, but all changes now. all changes but mother.

Waters are risin still, more each day. we all heard some great shift. all is change, but changes seem to root mother further down in to this place. as Waters rise, mother sinks. this is her place, it is her life and work. now it is drownin. she sees it and knows, but she will not change. mother was pillar of this place, guardian and leader. mother formin us all. now she is lost.

she walks bounds of great Cloyster each day now, Water lappin her feet, now comes up over roots of Cloyster it self. she walks and muttrin, she talks to Lady, offers prayers, but Birds will not speak to her, only father, and she does not know what to do.

sfia and i, we talked. we know mother, how well she will guard this place, how she would guard it with her life. she would fight any who threatened it, but she can not fight risin tide and she will not leave. she would rather go under Water. i will not go with her. i will not die for this place, and me girl will not. nothin will touch her. i would walk out now, go out in to world with me girl only. i would do this if i could.

we sat in Long Hall, el playin in corner with stones she brought from where edge of Water used to be. moorin places gone now, Bird Poles rise up from shallow Water. each day it may be one hand higher. it will not be long before this Hall risin from Water.

i will not leave, says mother.

mother, says sfia, gentle, *soon you will have nothin to stay for. Waters are risin daily, it is steady, it may be one or two weeks before there is no ground to stand on.*

we do not know that, says mother. *we know nothin.*

we know Waters will not stop, i say.

we do not, said mother. *we do not know why they rise, we do not know if they will stop. i am mother of this place, this is me ground, me work.*

sfia goes to mother then, neelin at her feet where she sits, takes her old hand in both of hers. speakin softly then.

mother, she says, *all you have done for Edg, all you have done for us, it is every thing. Lady knows what you have made and guarded, but all has changed now. father is gone, all are gone but us, now Land it self is changin. it is not wisdom to stay rooted if roots will drown.*

mother looks at ground, leans on her staff now. sudden she is old.

we must go, mother, i said. she looks up.

go where, nzil? she says. *go where? i have been here all me life, this Edg is where we made our stand. for eons we have been here. i am mother of this place. now some great shift is come. we all heard. this great sound, some thing movin deep. where will we go? am i to be last mother of this—*

she stops then. she can not speak further.

we can go to father, says sfia, *find him. you sent him seekin. he may have found.*

mother lookin at her for moment like she does not know where she is.

we can follow him, says sfia, *follow him west. to torr. hill will be above Waters. father may know what is happnin. you said, all have long gone to holy hill, for Truth can be found there. we can be together again. we can not stay, mother. you see this.*

for long time, mother only breathin. she closes her eyes. we wait. then lookin up like she has been spoken to.

it shall be like this, she said. *we shall ready cnoos, food and Water for journey. prepare and wait. if Water comes across sill of Long Hall, we will go. we will find father on hill and we will make things right again. we will find him, we will see what this is, we will return here and beginnin again. Alexandria will fall and we will begin again, in new world, free.*

yes, says sfia, *yes, mother, this is right. we will find father, make things right. findin Truth with him.*

it is right, i said also. i smile at mother. we will never return here. we will leave, we will not come bak. we all know this, and none speakin it.

as we moved away mother spoke, kept speakin, talks of this and then this, speakin to fill emptiness in her and to cover ground we headed towards. as if speakin would make sense of her leavin and make safe what we moved in to. we took long cnoo, filled and strapped down, nzil and i took paddels. el sittin on mothers lap, chattrin also, for her it is great adventurin.

mother did not look bak, not once, did not turn to see great Cloyster half drowned now in mere and Long Hall flooded and Water still risin below us. none speaks of what we left and will never come to again.

in short time all of us have gone further than any in our lives, further than we had ever gone to fish or pray. only father has travelled far and returned. we must follow trails and Stars and Birds and what mother knows of Land and we must hope we reach holy hill. there is nothin else now but world spreadin before us and all things in it.

Wind blowin today, Wind from west movin over Waters, we must push in to it. Wind is warm but strong, makin shapes on surface of Waters and sounds.

listen, says mother then. *sfia, nzil, stop rowin. listen.*

we listen. all around it is as if Waters whisper to them selves, as if beneath shiftin waves voices chattrin and sing. mother stopped talkin then, listens. we all hear it.

Water is speakin.

father once told me, mother said, *of distant Waters he jour- neyed over many years ago. only him, alone in small cnoo on great mere and as he moved he begins to hear strange sounds. he said,* Water was singin to me. *then he stopped paddlin, lettin cnoo hang on Waters, and he looks down through these Waters which were so clere and beneath, far beneath, he saw great ruins of city. he seen torrs, he said, torrs and walls and one great spire and voice seems to sing from spire, sounds pulled up from depths through spire to surface and then through in to air. he did not want to leave, he said, it was as if this old city was callin him, as if old, old voices from deeps call him to stay here, come down, join them, and he must make great effort to pik up paddel again and movin away.*

i pulled harder on paddel then, we moved on in to Water and sound was still there, chattrin, whisprin all around. after some time i stopped pullin, rest me arms, turned and lookin bak for last time at hill, at our Edg. i seen then Bird Poles risin from Water to Sky, work of nzils life now stitchin current to current with no ground between, last solid things in great flow which makes us small, pushes us on.

that night we slept in cnoo. it was hard to sleep, it kept rokkin and i was scared and happy at same time. it was amazin to be on Water, no Land round, only mere. i have never been any where i could not see Trees. i missed me Trees and me Birds. that day, paddlin without Land near, only Bird we saw was Gol, some times passin over head, cryin like he was sad. now at night, no Birds heard at all, only lappin of Water. mother, dada and mam were sleepin, pushed together close in cnoo.

i was lyin between them, but i could not sleep, it was wobbly. i sat up and lookin out at dark mere. it was still warm. it is always warm, even on Water. it was so dark! i did hear Water lappin but nothin else. no breeze, no Birds, and no Moon tonight. in Sky, Stars were like littel stones on fyr. i wondered if they would drop from Sky and in to cnoo. i would put them all in me littel leather bag, keepin them for ever.

then when i was lookin out at mere i saw Stars on Water. i looked for long time, careful because it was strange, but it was true what i saw. it was like littel orange Stars flotin on mere long way out. littel flikkrin lights. they did look like Stars but they were not, they were like littel fyrs made by people, like candels, and they must have been flotin because they bobbed like our cnoo. no body else sees them, and i did not say any thing in morn when people woke because i forgot. i dont know what they were. i think there are magik things out here. i wonder where we will go next?

all is strange in Stars now. in Stars and in air all around. i have not heard this in any stories or Dreamin. Water risin, still risin. if yrvidian were here, he could follow it in Dreamin. if father were here, i could send him to Birds. Lady will tell me in time. some thing is comin. it is like whole Erth has shifted.

will that thing follow? they always follow. we are few, but we can keep it off. it only has words. but what do we have? nothin left from what we were and built. only what we carry now, and what we are. only what we see.

three days we paddled, Flis and Skitos heavy in air, hot even at night. seein line of Land long before we come to it and when we came we saw great trunks of Trees, wide as Long Hall, standin in risin Water. no strand, no moorin place. we bring cnoo in to thik of Brambel and Bambu on floor of this great holt. we climb out, bring our food and saks.

we stand then, we fore, looking up at these great Trees, so tall and wide and silent as i have not seen. stillness and silence all around. there is buzzin of Fli and Skito and Mij, but no Birds, only great ringin silence of these things, risin now from Water.

come, i say, *let us move to higher ground.* nzil and sfia shouldrin saks, i take els hand, we push through windin Brambel and Thorn.

where now? says nzil.

look for signs, i say. *if they came this way they would have cut path. nzil, sfia, go searchin. i will stay here with el.*

i must sound sure for them, but i am not sure. i do not know this place. i am sure of nothin.

can i go too? said el. i saw nzil turn, puttin out me hand to steady his arm.

it is well, i said to him, and then to el: *no. you stay with me. woods are not safe.*

why not? she said. *what is here?* ah, this girl, her freshness, it keeps us alive, i think now, helps us keep movin, that we have some thing to move for.

they always tell me places are not safe now. ever since Catt and strange man i am not allowed to go any where. it makes me bored and fed up. why can i not look around wood with mam and dada? it is amazin new place, Trees are so big. Catt man will not be here, he could not follow us over Water. i played in holt for years at home and mam never cared where i was. she followed lorenso in to woods, but never followin me.

when mother talked about things not bein safe, i remembered lights i had seen on Water that night. i wondered what they were, so i ask her. her face goin funny and she sat me on her lap. every one is so serious now.

what did you see, girl? she said.

lights, i said, *like littel Stars, like fyrs bobbin on Water long way out.*

mother fiddlin with me hair then, tyin it up at bak where me pig tail has got loose.

some times, she says then, *there are strange people on these Waters.*

what strange people, i say. this sounds like adventurin. i

269

am not allowed in woods any more, and me Catt has gone. may be from Waters magik will come.

strange people, she says, old people. they live on botes, rarely comin to land. they have been here for ever, since before Wayland. long ago they took to Waters, keepin from Wayland and his stalkers, keepin away from all other humans. they are born and dyin at Sea, on meres, on rivers of this Land. they do not like us, do not want our type near them.

i think this sounds good. i would like to live on bote for ever. i dont say that though. i say: *can they hurt us?*

they may. we can not trust them. no body knows them. it has been said that they take children. for bad reasons, el, i will not tell you more. if you see lights movin on Water in that way it may be them. hungry ghasts, we call them. if you see this, you must say.

what will you do if they come?

i have things i can do. but you must say if you see any thing of this kind, el, do you see? do you understand? that man in holt, he could have harmed you. you must speak, speak out, girl. world is big, you see, with many strange things in it. they are not all nice.

she hugs me then, tight, like she thinks i am scared. i am not scared. i want to see all these things in big world. i do not want them all to be nice. i am not baby. i would like to see lights comin closer. i would like to see Catt again. mother huggin me so tight now, i think it is her that is scared instead.

soon enough we found their trail. they had hakked through Trees and vines and made small path. sfia and i we hitched saks on our baks and walkin together, mother and el comin last. walkin was hard, slow, even with cuts father made. we can see where his nife lands.

we walk west, as ancestors did. this is way of humans, i think, for all time. when all changes, walk west.

i feel like me lifes work is done. i have felt this since we began to move away. i saw me Poles reachin up to Sky. well, it may be they are offered to Sea now. it may be Swans will come. but i have done me work and i have done it well, done it with pride. now i flote and i will see what world bringin me. only one thing must i do now: keep me girl safe. i will watch her grow, easin her in to what world she will come in to. it is me last task. fathrin. hardest task and best.

we move slow, will take weeks. will we have them? we are deep in holt now, push through past great trunks of old Trees hummin low as we pass, singin to each other. we walk slow with young woman and old. we can not see Waters but they have been risin for weeks now. do they rise still?

first night we stop in small glade, eatin what we had carried, dry Yam and Tayto and salt Fish, drank what we could from skins. we have not yet found spring. el was sleepin almost before we stopped. light comin late this high summer.

in small glade was great Elder Tree. Elder of elders, bark lined as i am lined, limbs bent as mine are bent. old Tree he was, growin up to light as well he can. alone i stood with him, hearin deep hum in his veins, stood until i could hear it well, then i begin hummin with him. old Trees hummin deep, young hum high. we both stood in glade hummin song of this place, song that comes up from Clay and singin through long vein of all that lives.

i placed me hands on his bark, we stand then, Elder and i, and we hum song of this small place on Erth. i sink in to his song, matchin his tone with mine and in time we sing together, one song as one bein. his song is different from all others. twenty paces west, Trees will hum in an other tone. Erth is great map of song like this, great Land scape of tone and musik. when humans forgot songs, when they sang their own over all others, one song for all places, that was when great dyin began. always walkin, never listnin, we are. always goin west.

Ascension 481-K
L: Albion Q14 – Nitria/Holland – #20 'Sfia'
TD: Alexandria 237483830202/6988
Result: Ongoing
Transcript follows

Following the recent debacle, I resolved to concentrate instead on the mother of #19. I judge her to be more emotionally labile than her offspring; certainly she exhibits less mental discipline. She continues to lust after poor #18, whose form I took in drawing her attention as her party slept, on their first night on dry land. The response was, as expected, both immediate and enthusiastic. She followed me quickly into the forest.

Subsequent developments were less predictable.

Due to the unorthodox environment and situation, I would expect this ascension process to be more drawn out than others. I remain confident, however, that the result will prove positive.

*

Target: So this is what you are?

K: You do not seem surprised to see me.

T: I knew you were not Lorenso. You did not smell right. Is this how you lured him? Did you become me?

K: He spoke about you a good deal. Perhaps he still does.

T: Where is he?

K: In Alexandria. He has become part of the great human whole. His potential expands as we speak. What—

T: Poor boy. My poor, young boy. What did you do to him?

K: I only spoke with him, offered him a chance to be something greater than he was.

T: He was always on fire, always running. And now you think I will follow. Now you think I will follow for love of him.

K: I have faith in your reason. There is much I can tell you.

T: Ah, you strange thing. Look at you. What are you? Are you human, are you man, woman, animal?

K: I am one of Wayland's retainers. You may call me K.

T: I may hang you from tree for what you have done to my beautiful young man.

K: You are angry. You rage inside like winter storms.

T: I am many things you do not sense. Do you think you can play with me like you did to him? I know what you do. I am not young like him. What did you do with his body, his beautiful young body?

K: The body is an encumbrance. It is the mind that grows, pushes through. Wayland—

T: Where is it?

K: You should ask your father.

T: Father was there?

K: Rather too late, from his perspective. Perhaps he knows what became of the body of your lover.

T: Do you know what body is?

K: I know what a human is. I know the interconnected mass of tissue and blood, cell and bone, the map of lust and need. Each of you is a constellation of desires patterning the world. You do not know yourselves, or what you want or what you are. Your body drives you on, blindly.

T: Who is the me that is driven by this body? There is no me, no body. All is one. What could I take from what I am and still be Sfia?

K: Would you like to know? I can show you.

T: I would like to know what disease you carry, seeing splits where there is none.

K: A human is all division. A human is a thousand people fighting inside a bag of blood and flesh. You do not know what drives you, moves you, sparks your lust or anger. You do not understand a thing about what you are.

T: And you will tell me?

K: In Alexandria, all is clear. Take the mind from the body, walk out of the clumsy, messy shell and the spark is released. The minds there are like particles, always attracted to each other, feeding from each other, merging, endlessly evolving. Nothing is unknown, nothing is opaque, everything is clear, transparent like glass. Everyone is the equal of everyone else, kinks in individual minds are evened out by exposure to the whole, and the whole, together, is more productive than you could possibly imagine. Ah, what will be achieved there, Sfia! It is pure human potential, sheer as a red cliff at sunset. It is what God intended. Perhaps it is what God made.

T: You are like child. Strange, lonely child.

K: What are you doing?

T: I am coming to see what you are. See, here I am. Does it make you sweat, me standing this close?

K: I do not sweat.

T: How do you feel when my body comes this close to yours?

K: I feel nothing. It is of no interest to me.

T: Woman's body does not move you?

K: Woman, man, these are words. All is one.

T: Then why do you shrink back? Are you afraid to be touched?

K: You are wasting time with this sort of game. These nights are short. There is much I could tell you.

T: You poor sad being, you have never been touched! Here, placing my hand on your chest. Does it afear you?

K: Why would it?

T: Then why do you twitch? See, here is another, on your hip. Now, is my hand not warm on your body? Do you feel it, feeling me enclose you? Why do you stiffen?

K: Stop touching me.

T: I see you now! All your words, your fine speech, where does it go now? You want to leave your body because you do not know it. Poor child, they have bred you like some piece of meat. You are all ideas and words, you have never been held, never being loved, never fucked. You take my poor Lorenso to your dead city, and you did not even know what keeps him here.

K: Oh, I know, I know. I know the tuggings and the pullings, I know what they lead to. I know what you will do once you are on fire. I have seen it.

T: No, you do not know. You do not know because you have never felt it, never living it, only speaking and thinking. You are half in your city already, poor being. Once you are fully there, you will never feel hand upon you again, and you know, don't you, what you have lost? I feel it shivering through you.

[At this point it seemed prudent to retreat, given the target's unpredictable behaviour.]

T: Yes! You are afeared by your body! You are afeared by bounds, walls, limits. By your very skin, outline of yourself. You are afeared of all things you cannot be. You think that what limits you denies you. You do not see that bounds are what make you. We push against them, and they make us sing! Ah, and you are shaken. Poor creature.

You took my young man, you try to take my girl away. I should be angry with you, but I am only sad for all you do not know, all you cannot be.

[Now she places her hand on my face. I simply stand, allowing her to move as she will. It will pass. It is nothing to me.]

T: Do not be afeared. I am here.

we sleep in open place by some great old ruin, vined stone tooth growin in holt. strange thing it is. wakin early with summer light, movin on after small pieces of food. littel is left now. Water we have, as there is fresh spring here. but soon we will have to hunt. nzil and i have bows, nife. perhaps tonight we will set snares.

mother always wantin now to move. she has lost Edg, lost who she is. leavin it was like losin some part of her body, i think. world now is strange to her. and there is some thing else. she feels some danger is near. K is still with us, i am sure. he will visit me again.

but mother will have us walkin on, all day, as much as el can stand, like we could walk away from it all. she would have us out of this holt, again on Water. she feels safer on Water, i think. does she think father will save us, or Birds, or Lady, or is it only that she does not know what to do but move?

we will walk perhaps three more days, mother says, but it is not known. Water still risin, Land shrinks, heat sokin in to us. walkin west.

he will come again tonight i think, he will not give up. he must take us all there. all day i will think of lorenso, away in dead city. he has gone there and yet. and yet Dream tells us Swans will come bak, Alexandria will fall. then what will happen to me boy? i would like to ask mother, but what can she do?

i think i will have to do this with only me self.

Persistence, it is clear, will be the key with this target. It is not unusual for them to imagine, in the initial stages, that they can outwit or confound us. This resistance wears off after some time, usually defeated by simple curiosity. It is ultimately a primitive ego-defence, which cannot last.

I will visit her nightly until there is a resolution. I will not fail. I have no intention of spending any more time in this foetid swamp than is necessary.

I am also concerned by the environmental changes I am seeing. The rising of the waters is of a piece with an unusual vibration on the ether which became apparent during the ascension of #18. Wayland has not responded to my queries about this. I take His lack of response to indicate that a response is not necessary. He is taciturn at best. But still, it adds to my desire to be done here.

I have waited too long to see Alexandria.

*

K: You are awake.

T: You came back. I have been waiting for you.

K: Follow me.

T: I may follow you into woods, but no further.

K: Then come. We have not spoken seriously. Speak to me as we walk.

T: What do you feel as you walk?

K: What?

T: What do you feel? How does your body feel? When your feet stepping on woodland floor, feel of needles and leaf rot between your toes. Air in your chest.

K: We will move some distance away. We do not want to be overheard. There is much to tell you.

T: What is around you is also in you. You are not in holt, you are holt.

K: Do you know how many people I have sent up to Alexandria?

T: Tell me.

K: Four hundred and seventy nine. For years I have tramped around your little settlements, listening to your drivel about birds and dreams and the lady and the rest of it. Anything you can say to me now, I have heard before. I,

285

however, can tell you things you do not know; show you things you have never imagined. You have no idea how limited your portrait of the world is.

T: What is wrong with what I am? What is wrong with this body, this woman?

K: You are proud of that body, aren't you? You enjoy using it. You inhabit it well. But that is the trap. You identify yourself with your container. But you are more than that. The deeper you sink into identification with your limbs, your facial features, your embodiment, the less you will see.

T: I do not even understand your words. It is like you speak from some other world. Like you do not know where you are.

K: I know it better than you. Your body is a temporary container for something which becomes great only when released. Do you not have any desire to know what this means? Are you not curious to explore what you might become?

T: Poor creature, your body making you shiver.

K: Your lover knew. His body bonded him. It bonded him to you, and his lust for you was impossible to shake off. The poor boy, that lust defined him, dragged him down. It was like a shade he carried on his back. You did that to him, Sfia. With your beloved body.

T: Let me speak to him.

K: It is impossible. Alexandria is bounded. None may approach but through the gateless gate. There is no return.

T: Then he is lost.

K: He thrives. You could join him. I could show you how.

T: And then this body you speak of, all that I am, would be shed like some snakeskin in summer.

K: It would no longer bind you. This is what I am trying to tell you, Sfia. Raise your gaze from yourself for just one moment. Look at the big picture. I will tell you what I told Lorenso: the human body is a machine which damaged Earth so badly that it had to be controlled. Reined in. Wayland offers you a way to be yourself for longer than you ever could in this limiting frame, and then to rise beyond it. Alexandria is the saviour of both humans and the wider web.

T: Mother has spoken to me of your story. But you know ours also, so you know then that no war has ever happened in our order. No murder, no battling, no anger. We have lived on Edge for aeons, and seeing only peace. To follow Way is to live in world deeply. This we do, and you know it, for you watch us, we know that also. You come to me with tales that are lies.

K: It is true that your systems, on the surface, have been reasonably effective. This is partly because your numbers are small and your level of technological development is deliberately stunted. But it cannot last, you see. It never does. Eventually, something will break, from within or without. Your order has been living like this for centuries, and still there is anger, violence, lust in the hearts of your people, bursting to escape. It escaped from Lorenso.

T: He was young, poor boy.

K: He was human! This is what you *are*. Transcendence of your whims, prejudices, appetites, loves, hates, ideological confections, tribal allegiances – all of this is virtually impossible for you. Reason cannot conquer millennia of animality. Your history shows this: just at the moment when reason seems to triumph, you crash back again into barbarism. You suffer so much from simply being embodied. It is why we offer you the chance to leave it all behind. To come to a place where all is mind. Or spirit, if you prefer. But not meat. It is the meat of you which causes all of the bloodshed throughout your red history. Red meat: beneath your skin, this is what you all are. Red meat running.

T: Poor creature. Birds seeing you for what you are. Do you see rook circling over holt as we walk? He knows you for what you are. Little lost boy, wanders in wood talking, talking. All your words, and what is under them? Empty cauldron. Metal and air.

K: You people and your birds! I can take you to places no bird could go. I offer each individual the chance to transcend what limits them. I can free you from your bonds.

T: But I am not bonded, poor creature. See?

K: Are you going to touch me again?

T: Do you want me to?

K: It is a waste of your time and mine.

T: Then why ask?

K: I—

T: Wayland made your poor body, making it cold and still. But still He makes it of flesh. Still I put my hand on you and you glow. See?

[K: No response.]

T: You like this?

K: It is unusual.

T: Poor boy, your body is saying what your words do not. Now, another hand. How do you feel? Do you like it?

K: Enough of this. I have a job to do, and I am here to do it.

You may ask me anything you like. About Wayland, about Alexandria, about—

T: Tomorrow. Come and find me. Maybe I will ask. Maybe I won't.

K: You are leaving?

[Target departs.]

*

I will not pretend that this is not frustrating. It has occurred to me that it may be more sensible at this point to turn my attention to the lone male within the group. He is less impetuous, and seems less attached to the material plane. A cloud hangs over him. He would be easier to detach.

But I do not like failure. I will break through her carapace. And her hands are warm. It is a good demonstration of what keeps them here, in this wet, hot place. A good education. The warmth. Flesh is a strange and burning thing, a thorn. It sets confusion in the brain, it fogs the mind with the pulsing of blood. Flesh is the ink in the water of reason. There is no logic to it, no pattern that can be laid down.

There is ink in my water. Those warm hands.

I must be rid of this.

three days botin, three days walkin, now food runnin low. we have Water, springs are to be found now, but salt Fish will last perhaps two more days, and all Yam, Tayto and Notweed is gone. me girl will not hunger. what ever else this journey brings she will not hunger, not while i live.

tonight, when we stop, i will set snares. i do not like snares, do not like takin wights, but we must eat. what will come to them? Cony? Hair? i will not harm Hair. Hair is painted with Ladys colours.

strange feel to these old woods, not like holt near Edg. sounds i hear, they are not what i have heard before. we do not know what is here, what danger it brings. i have heard tales of beasts made by Man, put together from parts of others, let free to grow and hungrin.

they are only stories. still, i will keep me girl close. i have me bow, have me snares. we will eat, keep walkin.

mother says we may reach Water soon. we walk across great high spine of old Albion, headin to Afan Sea in west reach. when we come to Afan Sea we hope to find cnoos at moorin place that is called Lemtun. then we head south to find father. when we reach Sea it will be better for us. we know cnoos. all this walkin, this hakkin through, it is hard. el tires and food runs low. we sweat, wearyin.

we walked one more day today and this night comin to hill where Trees grow thin. Birk is here on tops, Alter near low, damp parts. hills are long, shouldred, makin me sik sudden for Edg, which rose also from wide Sea in this way. is Water still risin, is any thing left of our old place? what will our Order be without its ground?

creature moved with us all this day. i felt him in wood, shadowin. i was sad for him. he is like broken child. what is this world he builds? where will he go now?

he will go some where, for after this night he can not come again.

it was not long since i slept. Moon is waxin, her light fallin silent on leafs and trunks as we lay under Trees. always holt is writhin, day and night, always trekkin of wights through under growth, things in Trees, sounds.

things live here that humans do not see, do not know. holt is great writhin creature, we pass through small and with heads low.

i sat up when i heard sound for it was close and was not like any wight. noise was high and tight, like wight weepin. i stood and walkin in light of Moon and was led by sound in to Trees, not so far, and there it is, poor creature, it is caught in one of nzils snares. it sits on ground, sees me come, looks up at me. it looks like it weeps but it does not have tears.

i am caught, it says. *how am i caught? why did i not see? i could see all things, all was available to me, but now it is darker. Waters rise, Wayland is silent. some thing is wrong.*

i neel down by him and lookin at what had happened here. his foot is tight in snare set by nzil, wound around him and diggin in to his flesh. some blood comin out. it is like he has never seen blood before.

why did i not see? he says again. *where has me seein gone?*

i take his leg in me hand, i am tender but still he flinches.

i will be gentle, i say, *but we must take it off.* i begin unwindin snare from where it is caught, followin twine to unbind its knots. he makes small noises as i free him, but he says nothin until i have unbound his foot. he takes it in his hand, lookin at it like it does not belong to him.

meat, he says. *meat!* he passes one hand over his foot and i see nothin change but when i look his foot is clean, there is no wound.

thank you, sfia, he says. it is new voice for him.

i say: *body makes great pain, great joy. one sits within other. it is what life is.*

there are other lives, he said.

no, i say. *life and deth. this is all. it is why i will not have what you would offer me. what can human be without this blood, this pain? we are wights like any other. there is nothin to rise above.*

now it looks at me almost as if its eyes were human. almost as if some softness comin in to them, when before all it has been is some thing of air and metal with words that come from some height down to us.

i see you, he says. we both sit, still, on floor of holt. it is like he is human. *i see you, sfia. what you have is what i like about humans. there are things to admire, despite it all. you know, i regard you as my ancestors, you people here. i was once like you, i suppose, many generations bak. some times i think i can feel your pain. some times i wish i was as simple as you. i wish i could be so – uncomplicated. but humans have not been as uncomplicated as you for so long. you people do not know how unusual you were, even at your height.*

i say: *we know there are not many like us.*

there never were, my dear. all you resisters, even at your height, you were a tiny minority. i watched it happen. most humans chose the Machine, for it completed them. in an important way, it was the conclusion of all they had striven for for so long. as soon as it began to manifest, they grasped it hungrily. the Machine allowed them to take what was in their mind and paint pictures with it, real pictures. everything they could imagine, they could create. the great majority of humanity ran full pelt away from the messy, dirty, dangerous reality of the physical world and into what the Machine offered: the chance to make their dreams manifest.

yrvidian told me about Dreamin, i say. *he spoke of it once, though none could travel in Dreamin like he. he said,* Dream lines shine like spider strands in dew, and it is as hard to walk on them for they dissolve in comin of day. but Dreams are made, like webs, they are not born from within. Dreamin does not come from people, it is given by Lady. it is life of work to see this. *that is what he tells me.*

he would speak to me again but now comes other voice, movin from behind me, and i turn and there is mother. she pushes through Trees towards us, she carries her staff, she raises it like some prophet then and shoutin at us, at him, callin, *i told you, creature! i told you what would come! i will kill you, creature! you will leave us, leave my folk, i will—*

K turns to face her, calm now, like it is comforted by what it came for. it raises one hand, makin pattern with it in night air and mother then stops like she is Tree, like stone, stoppin as she ran, silent and still as if she was never human at all.

air, hangin i was then in air like Bird, but Bird with no body, no wings, i see nothin when lookin at me self but i am high in blu, hangin above great green island in wide morn Sea. beyond island is Land so great, so rollin that i can not see any end to it.

now i am fallin, fallin to ground so fast that i am in terror, afeart, but i feel nothin, no pain and now i am in Trees, in forest on this great island. trunks of Trees are so wide they dwarf any i have seen. they are wider than great Cloyster and Trees so tall their tops can not be seen. damp, brown like soil is air, sound of Birds so heavy it is like air it self is song. movin from Tree to Tree is Birds of colours so stark it is like they are made of Sun light. green and red and blu and yello they blaze and they sing in speech father could not understand. light and sound is like some dance of fyr and me hart soars, soarin for this fyr that reaches from Bird song, from Trees, roots in to me old hart.

now i see in holt some thing move and leafs part and great beast comin over to me. i am afeart but i have not body i am here but not here, it does not see me. great brown beast, paddin on in toward me and behind it now fore small ones come and they lay down and playin they are now like children. one rolls on its bak, other leapin on to it and pawin, bitin, fightin and mother then she sits on her haunch and watchin them play, likkin her paws as Birds callin over her like they sing great wild song of praise and now i am

up again up above Trees and i see this island and its great rivers, this huge Land with gold strands and plains and across plains flowin now great herds of some wight i have never seen, herds so great that plains shift from gold to brown and now i am down again and in to Sea, now under Sea, now deep in Water and Fish here are gold and green and patched and striped and bright as Birds, weavin through and round and in to forests of coloured stone and under Sea is world like i have never known and i am here now and would stay, would see more of this wonder i do not want to

K: Mother! How lovely to see you again. Did you enjoy Manhattan?

[The mother of the order, released, stands as if dazed before me and the girl. She leans on her old stick and glares, but the colours in her do not glare. They sing.]

Mother: What was that? What did you do?

K: That was life, mother. A little tour of the living Earth you know and speak of so well. I thought you might like to see what Wayland has achieved. You speak so ill of Him. I thought you should see the results of His healing mission.

M: You dare to speak of healing to me.

K: Of course, there is still much work to do. But wasn't it something? You have just visited what was once the heart of Atlantean society's greatest imperial centre. That island was a great human city. Steel, glass, smog, oil, millions of humans, always teeming, always growing. The continent beyond was all fields of grain, factories, railroads, more cities. The sky full of vehicles, the sea fished out, all the systems dominated by your kind. An impressive achievement in many ways. But now look at the change. We estimate another ten thousand years or so before equilibrium is reached. We have been able to accelerate the process significantly, but some processes we must leave to Earth. That is the point of this, after all.

M: I believe nothing you can show me. I know what you are.

K: Ah, the colours inside you belie your words, old woman! You know what you saw. You have felt it. I know what you think of me, and of Wayland, but I will tell you what I told your poor Lorenso before I released him: I do not lie. I am not permitted. I do not lie, and Wayland is no monster. If there are monsters on Earth, mother, they come in human shape.

M: You speak with forked tongue. You—

K: Yes, yes. But you know what you saw. Would you let humans loose on all that again? Trust that your Way and your bird poles would hold them back? Ah, I see the doubt in your heart, mother, even as you try to hide it from me. Yes, there! Even you know that the temptation to clear it all for farmland and hunt the big animals down again would be too much for any of you to bear. Don't feel guilty. It is what you are. You are as wild as anything else, as hungry, as territorial, and to repress those instincts, as you must in order to inhabit a civilisation, is not sustainable. They always come roaring out somehow, which is why your ancestors in the end lost their minds along with their bearings.

The body will do what it must, you see, mother. It has been Wayland's task to remove a particularly virulent invasive species from this planet, using methods which you would ironically refer to as 'humane'. Can you really tell me He has done wrong?

Sfia: You say that—

M: Silence, girl! For shame, this is your doing. You come to this creature at night, you think I do not see what you have done?

S: I—

M: Nothing from you! No words! As for you, creature – if I see you again, if I hear you, I will kill you. I do not care any further for rules. I will kill you.

*

At this point, the mother turned and left. Poor thing, I do feel for her. It is hardest for the true believers when the end comes. I have seen many of their colonies collapse and it is always this way. They see that they have dedicated their lives to a mirage. Many of them do not survive the revelation.

The girl's demeanour changed significantly too. She glanced at me briefly, then followed the mother into the wood. She did not say anything.

While briefly entertaining, this was not successful. And there is something else. A problem, perhaps. A glitch, at least. Either way, it disturbs me. As I transported her, as I called up the picture, I felt an unexpected resistance; something I have not experienced before. It was harder than it should have been. What is this?

I must contact Wayland. All will become clear, then.

In the meantime, my plans will have to change.

nzil wakes, el wakin, Moon throwin Tree shadows over them under skins on holt floor as mother comes ragin in and i behind her.

all i have worked for! she said, turnin on me, staff in her hand, wavin it now at me like some weapon. *all father has worked for, and you and lorenso would break it all! for your lust, your young, dumb lust, your itchin. do you think i have not seen it all? do you know how old i am, girl? i have seen it all, i have seen fools like you, worked all me life to rein you in. why do i do this, why? i work to contain fyr, you run and burn all with it! i should let you all burn! Edg is gone, Order is dyin and you play with me, you play with us? i should let him take you! go then! go to Alexandria, join your lover, you may all go, i no longer care!*

then she drops staff, sittin on ground in darkness and begin weepin. i have never seen mother weep. mother should not weep. and seein her now i feel some blak thing creep in to me. all Edg is gone but us and now mother, one who is pillar, is stone, is rok, goes too. i watch and can not speak.

now el comes to mother and she does not speak only sittin on her lap and holdin her, holds her tight, and mother holds el and sobbin slow in stillness of blak night, they rok, rok together.

one small Cony in snare last night. found him this morn eyes wide, pullin from me, but he could not get free. i wanted to untie him, let him limp bak in to holt. terror in his hart comin in to mine, he spoke with his eyes. *free me, brother*, he says, but he knew why i came. here is curse: we must eat, and this is what Erth burns for. we should live on light and air, there should be no pain.

i come bak in to sleepin place with Cony hangin from me hand. mother has not slept since last night but she is still now. light comin up over Trees but el sleeps on. it is like some thing has gone from mother, some flame that kept her. she seems older now. she has always been spear, always fyr. mother has held together all of Edg with love and fear. now she must hold her self. it is harder.

i sit by her, put Cony on ground.

we have food, i say. she looks at me, smiles gentle. *thank you, nzil*, she says. *soon we will come to Afan Sea. there will be Fish, we will eat. no more snares.*

now sfia comes to us. it is like she was waitin for some other to come between her and mother. she sits with us, mother between us now on ground, Sun comin up over wood. holt buzzin, heat heavy in air already. smell of leafs openin, ground breathin.

sfia says: *mother—*

it is well, says mother, and she says it slow like she is empty of fight. *it is well, sfia, that you spoke with it and did not go. it came to you, you did what you must. i am angered that you did not tell me, but it is done. these are hard times, we must come together.*

i do not think he will come bak, says sfia. i have not heard her voice so small.

it will, says mother. *it will come until we are all gone. it does not want me. i am too old, i can not bear young. it wants you and nzil, and el most of all. it must break chain, end line. it will come bak. in what shape we do not know. please, i speak to you both, me children. for all we have done together and been, i ask you now: speak freely to me. do not hide, do not keep any thing under. that is how they work. they divide, sowin seeds of fear, doubt, lust. in mind, in word, in Machine is deth. this thing brings deth. what ever it says to you, that is what it bears. see what became of lorenso. speak with me, for i am still your mother.*

we sit and watch light grow in Trees. Cony growin cold in me lap now. i said: *where now, mother?*

on, she says. *there is island, hill, torr in hart of Afan Sea. it is holy place. father is there. Birds speak with him. he will have news. he will know.*

what will he know? says sfia.

what is comin. what we must do.

i was so pleased to see Water! it is blu again. we have walked for days through holt. or it may be weeks. i dont know. every day looked same. lots of walkin, big Trees, very hot. i am tired and me feet hurtin. some times dada would carry me on his bak. i like that. i pretend he is wite horse and i am faery rider. *giddy, giddy!* he wont run though, he says i am too heavy.

but today we come to huge mere. it is like home again but not so big. at home you can stand on edge of holt and lookin out at Birds flyin round Greenrok in big circle and Sea goes on for ever. here Sea is big but you can see Land on other side. hills rise wite and green from mere. i wonder what is there? do people live there? or some other things? i wonder if we will go.

i miss Greenrok. missin me Birds. Birds here are not same. Gol is here, and Cro, it is true, and on flats here is Dipper and Catcha and Hern. but they are not our Birds in some way. i dont really know what i mean.

we felt Water before we come to it. you can taste Water in air. Trees got smaller and thinner and then we come out on to strands of sand and mud. they are so long! Water is comin up them, you can see it, once they must have gone down to Sea for miles, but they are still here. i ran on to sand and started playin. i love sand. there was not too much sand at home. i started making castel while they all went lookin for cnoos. some times i wish i had some one to play with, but other times i like bein on me own, with sand and Trees and Birds.

funny thing happened when i was playin. i was on strand makin castel and diggin mote with me hands. sand under me nails all soft and warm. i looked up at holt where we had come from, i dont know why, and there is Hair sittin. big Hair it was, just sittin at edge of Trees lookin at me. i sat and smilin at him, i say, *hello Hair!* then he lollops towards me on his big bak legs, he comes closer and i saw his wite tummy and blak tops of his ears, and he is lookin at me. it is very strange thing but when i look in to his eyes they look like eyes of person, not Hair. it is like i am lookin at human, not wight and he is lookin at me too. Hair lookin at me for while and i look at him and it is like we are both stuk until from air comes call of Gol, screams above and circles. i look up to see him and when i look bak i can not see Hair any where at all.

we left el on strand where we could see her and walkin along sands, north first, then south, lookin for cnoos. nzil said father had come this way, his cuts were still in Trees. father would have found cnoo here, it may be there are others. mother says this was once place where people come from all over, tradin, meetin, movin between. there would be cnoos comin, tied up, left for others. in high times of our Order this was crossin place for Nitrian folk, and in Atlantean times it was old city of Lemtun, which can be seen still in ruins in holt. when we come through to strand we see strange shapes in woods, great broken roks loomin where no rok should be, strange flat places, dips and torrs all covered now in moss and creepers. we walk through fast for there is no luk in these places, only deth comin to those who disturb bones.

i wonder if K follows. i feel like talkin with him again. if mother had not come i would have said more. if i had laid me hands on him two more nights what would he be? there is human in there. his words are like veil, behind them is scared child with no mother. his flesh wants to be in world, his words want to take him from it. he thinks he is above and beyond, but between his toes is mud. i have not seen him, not heard more. if he comes, i dont know what mother will do.

still, i would like to see him. is this wrong?

now there is call up ahead from nzil and we go to him. he has found old cnoo deep in bank, layered in reeds. we pull it out and lookin it over. it has been here years but we see no holes, it is wood not skin, well made. there is one old paddel. we will go south.

it was nice to be on cnoo again. it was bit wobbly today. dada was up front, there is only one paddel, but this mere seems to flow where we are goin. we are goin south, mam says, to find father.

it is excitin to be here. i dont know why adults are not excited. they look tired and mother lookin all round, holdin to her stik as we move, like she is scared. i dont know what could be scary here. we are out in great blu lane of Afan Sea, flotin down, Water is so bright, it flashes, light on it comin from Sun. i can see yello lines of sand all down edges and then holt risin from strand. on other side, where we have not been, i see hills goin up, they are light green, rollin, they look like they would be fun to run around, sleepin on. i think you could sit on one of those hills and lookin at Stars so bright these nights with Moon low now and it may be you could reach Stars, pull them down and keep them to light you in sleep.

Birds is all over us as we move like they are guidin us. Gol followin us as we go, Catcha pipin from shores to tell others we are comin. this morn we saw huge flok of Storlin comin over from one side of Sea to other, from one holt to other, it went on and on, Sky was blak and thrummin with them. mother smilin and callin out to them as they pass, *brothers! sisters!*

we seem to be movin fast. i asked mam if there would be any other people we could meet but she says there is none. she says if i see any thing on Water that looks like people i must tell her. if i do not she will be angry. she always talks like this and her eyes dartin about. when i am adult i am goin to not worry about dumb things. i am goin to play in sand and sleepin on hills and in Tree branches and not just talk all day about serious things.

day was long and i did not have much to do and got bored soon. mam started rowin and then dada put line over edge of cnoo and pullin out some Roak to eat. mother said we could stop tonight and light fyr to cook them. i hate raw Fish. for lunch i had some dry Fish again. i am fed up with it. i hate it now. they made me eat it and then i went to sleep for bit. i dont know how many days we will paddel.

i woke up because adults were all talkin. i saw that light had changed, Sun startin to dip down, even comes. Water is darker, not blu now, grey and with lines of red and yello and other colours comin from Sun and dimpsy light is comin, day becomin night slow. mother and mam and dada all lookin out over Water to far bank and i sat up and then see what they see. it is most strange thing.

over Water these great wite sheets are hangin, lots of them, and they move slow up and down like they dance on Water. two of them, then three, then more, they are like great sheets, very wide, much wider than cnoo. they are not Birds or wights, it is nothin human and it is like they dance. comin up from Water and waft about then go down in to Water again. they dont care about us, it is like they live here and are dancin. it is so strange. we all look and no body speaks, all just watchin. it is not scary. great dance of these things goin on as light goin down.

what is it? i say. mother turnin then to look at me like she did not know i was there. now she puts her hand on me lap and holdin me hand. *what are those things?* i say.

i do not know, she says. *humans are gone from these places. older things are comin bak. all is changin, always. it is not for us to know. only watchin.*

it is girl i worry for. sfia, she will be well. all things she can turn to her purpose. nzil, he does his work steady. i am too old to care what happens to me. but el i care for.

we come tonight to Land at dusk. these strange things we saw over Water, it made me see this place for what it is. this is not our Land. Edg is our Land. i knew it, could walk every inch and see what was. i knew each Bird, each Tree. but here i know no thing. me feet move as they always have but what do they move on? Trees here hummin different song.

we come to Land at dusk, haulin cnoo up high in to rushes. Water still risin, flowin over roots. in west tonight was thunder, rumbles low and far away. we stopped here for it looks low and flat and when we came in to shore we see why. small path leads from strand through stand of low Birk and beyond is small rise where grass is low. in this place stood circle of great stones. buried in Clay, crouched over like bent people, some lyin, some stand tall, grey and patterned in Likun, yello, grey, wite. these stand in many places across island it is said, though i have never seen them. they have been here for all time, since before Atlantis.

but it is not old people laid these new flowers on top of stones. it is not old people who have lit fyr in centre of circle, not old people drapin stones with vines which are hard now and yelloed. it is not old people hangin from Trees here patterns of Star and cross. when i see this i want to get bak in cnoo, leave, but nzil looks close, and he says these are some weeks old it may be, they are not fresh.

hungry ghasts have been here. they come to Land to worship in places like this. what do they worship, what angry god? what sacrifice? they move on these Waters, i feel it. i fear for us. fearin for el.

sfia makes fyr in circle where ashes lie, we cook Fish, eat. nzil will sit up this night, keepin watch, listen. we will see them if they come. we will have warnin. i have fought off this creature Wayland has sent, i will fight off any other thing. i will lose no more of me folk.

strange place it is, but i like it. great fleets of Duk, Drake, Morrun, Gol, movin on Water with us, flowin slow south. Some times Cumrant seen over head. Fish leapin at dawn and try light, and strange things also, like these wights we see last even, like flowers and fyrs in circle of stone. it is like some other world here, same but not same, and we are passin through. i am happy only flotin. i am free.

mother thinks it may be one more days journey to where father will be. we will see it, she says, we will see from many hours away. green hill risin from Waters, on top of hill is torr, and this is where he will be. any man who is to become father must spend time there, along with Water and Birds. when trouble comes, answers may come from there.

what if they do not? i said to mother some time bak. *what if there are no answers there? what if father has nothin?* she says nothin to this. mother is strained here, she is out of place, she is like bow strung taut. i have brought me bow and some arrers for i do not know what we will see or what will see us.

i would like to keep movin, beyond fathers torr, out to Sea. i would like to take cnoo all round island, round whole coast of Albion, up rivers, in Land. i do not care for any answers father may have. Waters keep risin, all changes and this is good. change must come and will not be stopped. i have made me Poles, done me work. now i would like to take el and sail away.

mam nudgin me and sayin, *el, listen, Night Gail!* it is lovely song. mam lookin bit lonely then. there is lovely strand on this bit of Land stikkin out in to Water like long finger. there is only littel bit left, because Waters are still goin up. we have seen lots of Trees with Water up their trunks, roots in Sea. i wonder if they like it?

adults are lookin at Land so they do not see what i see when i look bak. there are lights on Water again. they are far out and bobbin but it is like there is line of them like i saw before. they flikker like candels or fyrs, they are afyr in light. i watch them and they spread out, like there is more of them. it is like they are far out to Sea but they are comin closer. i am sure they are comin closer.

i dont tell mother as she would be cross. i wonder what they are.

it is hard for me to speak of what happened on that Land, on that finger of green in uncalled Water. of what came. not all is clere in me mind. nothin is clere now in me mind. some fog is on me.

ah, i do not know what is left now, what is even left of this life.

when we stopped, adults got all busy gettin out skins from cnoos and makin fyr. dada took his bow and arrers and went off in to holt to see if he could find any wights, for he had not caught any Fish that day and he knows i do not like any more salt Fish. yuk to salt Fish.

i asked if i could go too but he said it was not safe. so i sat on strand and watchin dark comin and lights on Water comin closer also. strand was lovely, there was Water on nearly all sides for this is thin bit of Land stikkin out in to Sea. Birds goin still now. lights are bigger, still flikkrin, still bobbin. still comin closer.

it is all me, all of this is me. i did not see them comin until they were close. we were turned in to Land, workin. el was on strand but she did not speak and then i stand and turnin and their lights are all around, on three sides and it is them.

they have come. rafts of them. hungry ghasts.

o, i raised me staff, i called. i screamed out at them, i promised them pain if they come to shore. sfia is screamin for nzil to come with bow. if bow was here we could keep them away, but he is gone with it in holt i do not know how far.

i raise me staff, i raise it but it feels heavy and i feel heavy and i do not see in me mind what came then. i do not see it even though each minute since then i have tried to draw it out from within me.

i am in fog. i can not see what they did. all i see is what we have lost.

mother has been speakin of hungry ghasts since we first left Edg but i have not listened much. she tells tales of harm they do, of what they want, we have seen signs of them. we all heard stories as children. *they take children,* mother would say around fyr. *take them, cuttin them up, makin sacrifice. they are beasts, they love nothin but their cnoos, they find human children, givin them to their gods. if you ever see lights on mere, run, tell us.* i did not really believe it. we thought it was just tale to scare us.

now they came, all around us now they were, six rafts comin in on all sides of our spit of Land, lashed trunks, masts in centre. on these rafts small fyrs burnin in bowls and people with long poles pushin rafts in to Land, towards us. they would not come in. it is said they never come to Land but to worship. they live, bearin young, die on these botes.

night is darknin now but for their lights and our small fyr. they are nekid all, long hair down, long beards, matted, they look so strange, they are silent, gathrin round us like they want to see, to stare, to know what we are. like we are wights they have not seen before. men on rafts leanin on their poles, womyn standin lookin, great breasts hangin down. rafts bobbin on Water all around us and i join mother now, i call, *nzil! nzil!* for he has bow and arrers, he could drive them away, but he does not come. they stare and stare like they are measurin us.

but he does not come and we stop callin then. i think we do not feel like speakin. all is slow then, we tire, we want to sleep i think but i can not see in me mind how it happened. it was like some spell, o i can not say, i can not say any thing more about this world, it is not me world, i do not want it any more, i do not want any thing but sleep. o me girl, me girl, me littel girl.

they came all around us
it was very still
there was one man on this littel raft and one woman
he was lookin at me for long time
raft comes in to strand so it almost touched
then he held out his hand to me
it was still every thing was still
mother and mam and shoutin for dada but sound was very
dim
like it was under Water or far away in Trees
no, they were shoutin, *leave her, no, el, do not*
nzil, they were shoutin, *nzil*
but they did not come to me
they could have taken me arm and pulled me bak
but they only stood
and he is reachin out now to me
his hand is turned up and now is still
it is still it does not grab me
it is like he is offrin or askin
like he was sayin, *come*
and i could hear him, though he said nothin, i can hear him
come, he was sayin, *come with us*
his eyes were kind
they were both still shoutin at me, but not movin not
comin
they did not come to help me

324

his eyes were very kind
it was not like they said it would be
he did not pull me he did not hurt me
he was askin gently
come, he said, he was askin
kind eyes
kinder than mams
i began to walk
i stepped on to raft and it wobbled
takin his hand
his hand is dry and small
he closed his hand on mine
he did not make me go i wanted to
i wanted to see
now theyre screamin but still did not move
why didnt they come if it was so bad?
lights flikkred about
shadows on Trees were really big
we were big shadows
Bird went over but i did not see
there was woman like him on raft
she was smilin it was not like they told me
now i turned to look at mother and mam as i climbed on
raft
theyre just standin
not screamin but still not comin for me
i wondered if they loved me
after all they said
i climbed on raft and sat next to woman
she is so thin

and she was lonely i can feel it
now she placed Dear skin on me
she was gentle
now man takin long pole out of mud and started to push
no body was rushin it is all slow
slow like Water at fenn edge
light and shadow and Bird comin over again
and we moved away
out to Sea

always i will see nzil until i am gone. always i will see him runnin from holt, his screams. it was like his comin broke some spell. mother and i standin on strand, their rafts movin away and littel el, me littel girl is with them and why did i not stop them, what is this, what mother am i?

then nzil he comes runnin from edge of holt and we turn at his cry. he has seen, he drops his bow and arrers he is screamin, *el! el! me girl! me girl!* he pushes me out of way, he throws him self in to Water, he swims out, tryin to reach them, but they are far now, they move fast, they are lights and he can not reach.

o i thought he would go like lorenso but he comes bak. he comes bak to shore drippin and he rises from Water like some beast and grabbin me by shoulders and screamin at me now. *you are her mother!* he screams, *her mother! you stand here! both of you standin. they took me girl! our girl!*

mother looks at him like she will cry.

i did not see, i say. *i did not – i –*

now he drops on to strand and he weeps like he has no hart left, like all that he was dissolves in to night sand, and now i weep too and mother. we weep with sand, with Sea, as last light goin out to west over blak Waters. he says, *me girl, me littel girl, me girl* over and over and over and each word diggin in to me hart like nail and has not left, will never leave.

and then he rises and on his face is this fierce light. last thing i see of me man is this fierce light and he looks in to me face and in to mothers. then he is speakin to us low, so low but such anger.

you let them take her, he says. *me girl. our girl, sfia! you let them take her!* now he is screamin again: *you are her mother, you let them, you let them!*

i could not speak, i am frozen now, i can only say: *i* –

but he turned then and saying nothin more, he turns and pacin steady and strong bak in to woods, and he cries, callin, shoutin so loud, he bellows like wight as he goes in to holt and we hear him until he has walked so far that sound is drowned by blak of night and then i hear me man, but i see him no more.

stalker! he is callin. *come for me! take me, red one! take me away!*

SHELL MOON

could be twenty days i have been in this place but it seems i have never come or gone. seemin like i was born and will die here. i would like that. seems i am hermit now, seems i have always been, seems me time at Edg was in an other life.

when i came to holy hill i saw no sign that any had been here for some time. no fyr ash, no beds in torr. torr is seen for miles as me cnoo comes down Afan Sea. risin from dawn mist i first saw it, streaks of red in Sky, mist hangin in bands over Waters, and then i see islands. groups of islands all over, scattered through Sea, and at their hart, like hart of old maze, rises tallest, ridged like great old wight, like Sir Pent curled around old World Tree. torr hill. this old stone torr on summit is older than Atlantis. fathers have come here for eons to listen, fast, strip world away, be given speech by Birds, Her servants. see what must be seen, always alone.

which father was last here i do not know. could be i am last father of this Order in all of world. but world is bigger than i can dream. Birds have told me this. no small body is big enough to dream world.

i have littel and this is good. have me mat to sleep on, line to catch Fish, bottel to hold Water, stone to spark fyr. i am alone with old stone torr and Trees that grow up to it on this hill that rises tall from mere like glass. and each day since i was woken by hill shakin, by great, low, silent sound from earth it self, by Sir Pent shiftin down below, each day since then Waters have come higher. trunks of Trees that grew on strand when i come here now are under Sea. still it rises.

Birds have told me why.

Ascension 481 was abandoned. She would not come to me again, and I would not risk violence from the mother of the order, whose mental and emotional fragility appears to be deepening. I resolved to turn my attention therefore to my final remaining target, the partner of 481 and father of 480. It was clear enough what strategy should be employed with him. I had the lure ready.

In the end, it was not needed. He came to me, as I waited in the woods. He came running, demanding, shrieking like a beaten dog. The trauma he had recently suffered brought him to me clean, but it was necessary to scrub him of the residue. This was not swift work. It took me much time to calm him enough to even begin the necessary preliminaries. I explained to him that ascension was not possible in an emotionally fraught state. The mind must be calm, the motives clear, the decision well informed.

We spent time on this. I talked much. Over three full days we walked further into the woods on that barren little finger of land, far away from his people. We walked and talked and when I judged that he was ready, we began the process.

But something went terribly wrong.

I do not know what to say, or what is happening. Nothing like this has ever occurred to me, or to any retainer I have known. I have not seen it in any of the records. It is, I am convinced, unprecedented.

It was not my mistake. I am sure of it.

I performed the preliminaries, but I received no response from Wayland. I did not know why. It was unusual, but I continued. A personal response is not strictly necessary as long as the channels are open, and I believed I was experienced enough to know how to manage all eventualities.

Here I must be honest: I fear I hurried the process, for my own reasons. I fear that my own desire to leave this cursed ground, to meet my quota and take my own place in the city, led me to behave in a manner less cautious than was seemly.

I do not know. All I know is this: we began the process. His mind left him, it vaulted the gap, took to the diastolic channels, began the journey. But something happened. Something happened and I cannot say what. I cannot say what happened or what the result was. I cannot say where he went, or if he went anywhere. All I can say is that his body remained with me, empty; dead, if you like. The body remained, the mind left, but it did not follow the usual course. It did not progress along the predetermined route. It did not reach the gateless gate. There was no response, either from Wayland or from the watchers on the threshold.

It was as if the roads to Alexandria had changed course, or been blocked, or rerouted. Something had shifted. Something huge and fearful had shifted.

I sent him up, but the city was not there.

i did not seek. those who come to torr may not seek, must not ask. ask is not answered. if Lady will speak, Bird will be sent. if not, there will be nothin. i was sent here by speakin wheel, Birds sent me west. i knew they would come. i only waited.

each day risin with dawn, lookin out over old mere of Avlon, hart of this holy isle, seein mists comin up over old places. i sit, old legs bent under me, mind empty, thoughts blown by any breeze comin. sittin until ready, then down hill in silence, no speakin, in to cnoo, out to Sea. over old drowned city of Glasbri, Fish is found in plenty. it is best place. some times, not so far down, old torrs, walls, streets are seen, driftin now in time like Waters holdin me. i take only what i need, then sittin in cnoo, some times for hours, listnin, still.

it was six days, i think. by this time i had shed skin of old father, shed skin of Bird speaker of Edg to far east. now i was only man, small old man with no name, no place, sittin on hill legs crossed, Sun goin up, Sun goin down. nothin to say, no person to be. i was ready.

at dawn, Hern comes from far west. i see him through mist climbin up from Sea. Hern comin over me, Hern, lord of Places Between, wing beats hissin, legs hangin heavy.

Hern lights on top of torr, lookin down. all other Birds
silent then.

make circle, says Hern. *ancestor circle. tonight. he will
come.*

who will come?

he will come. be ready.

Afterwards it was unclear what I should do. Repeated attempts to contact Wayland met with no success. Wayland is not communicating. This is unprecedented.

What have I done wrong?

I have so few remaining before I can ascend. I am so close. It is cruel. If I cannot ascend, what do I do? Where do I go? What has it all been for?

I remained in that part of the woods for twenty-four hours. I balanced myself, ensured I was calm, ready. I continued to attempt contact with Wayland, and continued to receive no communications from either Him or Alexandria. Not only can I not reach Wayland, I can contact none of His other retainers. There is no procedure for this. We do not prepare for it because it is not possible. It would be like preparing for gravity to suddenly stop working. Silence on the grid is a physical impossibility.

I could have waited for longer, but at what cost? I need to move. I need answers. I must ascend. I must reach Alexandria. It is all that I am, and have been, all I have worked for. I must leave this muck, this rotting, warring place. I must reach the light. It is the promise that keeps me, that holds me in all.

If Wayland will not speak to me, there is only one place I can go.

i watch for dusk to begin gathrin far away. i saw it clustrin first in east, and beginnin me work then. in torr when i came was great heap of dry wood gathered in past by others. i made fyr in ash outside torr. i had gathered stones, branches, cones, wood from holt all day. now i lay it out in circle around fyr, around me. i will be safe in here.

i light fyr as dark comes in from west.

pacin circle then, makin it safe. then as fyr rises i neel by it, i face west. for Lady of rushes i bow me head. i offer to each of fore directions. what will come will come.

fyr blazes high and dark comin in now so that what is beyond circle can not be seen but in shadow. red light of fyr throwin shapes out on to hill. air dancin now, figures passin by. breeze comin and goes.

they do not come in. none can come in. shapes move outside circle. more of them now.

i stand then and callin: *ancestors!*

hands raised then, i call: *ancestors! those who stand silent at me shoulder! those who stand in long line behind, walkin bak through time. those who have made me, human and wight, all beins who have made me, i call on you. i call on any who would aid me.*

come!

i am ready!

speak!

hands lowered then. outside circle, shapes still passin, movin, flikkrin. fyr high now. me eyes look out beyond any movin things, focus on dark it self, on no thing. lookin as if through Water at what is below.

arrers comin down now from Sky, arrers up from ground to meet them, and warm red Sun in Sky though Sun has gone and night is here. now flikkrin, dancin sheet of light, green, yello, red, wite, hangin down from Sky. Lady of rushes, green Lady, wite Lady. all colours dancin now and some thing movin round circle.

now some shape, some human shape, movin in darkness. now it comes closer, to edge of fyrs light, lookin through me as if i am not here. he is old, bearded, shinin in light of fyr in silver helmet, green cape, he holds great sword with great anger, now steppin towards me but dissolves at circles edge.

now some other man, younger, thin, nekid in light, pale, bruised, damaged like he has hung up on Tree for vision.

in his eyes no anger only askin. he too steppin through fyr and is gone.

now comes new sound, sound like crakkin and it is behind me and i turn. fyr burning slower now, burnin small and beyond is dimmer and shape passes edge of circle like Dog, great grey Dog. now some blak Bird movin in Sky and now one other man he stands at edge of circle, still as stone.

holdin staff, one eye only under great hat he wears and this eye it looks at me, he says no words this one. oldest of old ones, he says no words but in his eye is all what i have come for, in his one eye is Truth, in his one eye is Edg, Alexandria, Wayland, what has been, what will come, what this is, who i am. nothin is said and i see all.

now i see all.

now i know Swans are comin, and now i know why.

I have lived to free people from their bonds. Only now do I begin to understand those bonds. I begin to taste the stock at the base of primitive humanity. These last few days, it was as if I were thrown back to pre-Atlantean times. I was unable to access any small part of the grid. No answers were given to any of my questions; no directions; no guidance. Wayland remains silent.

Research is impossible, the entire grid is dark. The silence is the worst of it. The silence is like a wound. All I hear is birds, water, wind. No conversations, no guidance, nothing to carry me and hold me as I move. Nothing human. I am alone with the world.

I have been forced to navigate by the stars, what little I know of them. The river carries me south. I am at its mercy.

This morning I came in sight of my goal.

I will have answers.

day is hot as all days are. Water still risin. each day i come down from torr, walkin down slope to see levels. each day perhaps one or two hands it has come risin. i watch with interest. it will find its level. it is not given us to know what that will be, or if we can live with it.

i knew he would come. i stand on summit and lookin at mere and his cnoo comes, spek at first in great Sea. i did not know when i first saw it if it was mother, el, sfia, and me hart leapin then. but as it comes closer i see it is lone figure.

i thought he would come. what else does he have now?

i light fyr and wait for him. his cnoo comin closer on light breeze. Sun is high. i cook two Roak on spit, turnin them, leave them to wait in ashes. he will be hungry.

i see him come in to Trees. i wait. then from Tree line, comin up slope towards me, he comes. thin he is now, drawn. he comes slow, unsure. he does not look in to me eyes until he stands before fyr.

father, he says then. his voice is smaller.

creature, i say. *welcome to Avlon.*

do not call me that. i am human also. i have hart also.

human, are you, now?

in all things that matter, father, we are alike.

how you have shrunk, me friend, without Wayland to carry you. your words are smaller.

what do you know? he says. lookin in to me eyes then.

Fish is good. that is what i know. sit, if you will.

he sits then, like small child, foldin legs under him. i pass him spit.

eat, i say.

Being here is strangely comforting. It has calmed me a little. This is not something I ever thought I would say. Naturally I would give anything for the grid to light up again; for Wayland to communicate. I would give anything to be in Alexandria.

But it is some comfort to have company, even of this kind. Since the silence of the grid, the absence of Wayland, the loneliness has been deep. It was not a word I ever understood. Now it fills me with sorrow for all who have known it.

If Wayland were to ask me why I had come here, my answer would be clear and arguable. In the absence of instruction or guidance, remaining with my targets is the sensible choice. The old man and woman are not on my list. But the others will come. It will be possible to readjust the systems, to compensate for the errors. When Wayland is ready, He will speak to me.

In the meantime, the old man speaks with me instead. He seems calmer than he was. It is harder for me to see him without the grid. I cannot see within. But I sense that there is less anger in him. Less melancholy too, perhaps. There was always melancholy in him, this one. I found it one of his most appealing characteristics. It hung around him like a cloud which he struggled sometimes to see through. I would have told him: there is only one way to escape this. Like all moods, it emanates from your body. It ties you to your frame as if by a rope to your belly.

But I am not sure about these words any more and this one, in any case, would not listen. He will go nowhere until the Earth takes him away. He is rather admirable in his stubborn refusal to attend to reality.

The fish is good. The day is hot, the fire hotter. He looks out across the water regularly. He is waiting for them. He begins speaking, his eyes still casting around the wide horizon.

Why are you here, K? he asks me.

I am waiting.

You are waiting for my people, so you can take them away?

I do not know, father, what I am waiting for.

I see something in your eyes which was not there before. Something in your voice.

Perhaps.

You are afeared. You have been abandoned.

No.

I think so. Waters rise and all things silent with you. You came to us so full of your city, so sure. Now you are not sure.

Things are changing, it is true. All is not clear. But Wayland will make it clear.

If it were not for the pain you have caused my people I would feel for you. What is your work now?

It is the same.

But you cannot do it. All is changing. Wayland has abandoned you.

No.

Perhaps Wayland is dead.

Wayland cannot die.

People made Him. People could unmake Him.

You do not understand what Wayland is. You do not understand at all.

Then tell me. We have all time. Sun shines, Waters moving. We are alone. Tell me your story.

I stand up, then. I stand and stretch my tired frame. Suddenly, I feel so tired. I walk to the summit of the hill and pace around the perimeter of the stone tower. I see nothing in any direction on the waters but birds. Hundreds and hundreds of birds.

I am sick to death of birds.

I return to the fire, which is burning lower now. It is absurdly hot even without it. The father sits cross-legged next to it. I sit again.

Tell me what you know of Wayland, I say.

Ah! he says. *You return to what you were made for.*

Tell me, father, please.

You know what we know. Why do you ask?

I want to hear your story, from you.

Wayland was made by people to build Alexandria. We made Him so we could live forever. Oldest dream. To be gods.

And how did people make Him?

How would I know this? Nobody knowing this.

I know. All retainers know. All of the history is revealed. We know how Wayland came. It is not what you think.

Tell me, then. I will listen. I am not busy.

Neither am I, father. We share that. And you should know how it was. You have travelled far.

Tell me.

Wayland's creation was a long process, father. There were plenty of false starts before they really understood what it meant to bring into being a mind that was not human and was not animal. That was what they were after, back then: they were trying to build minds. Intelligences was the word they liked to use, though it was the wrong word. Back then, they believed they could create an intelligence greater than themselves. They made plenty of monsters this way. Some of the resulting mess had to be cleaned up by Wayland when they finally figured it out.

What do you mean?

They came to see that intelligences cannot be created by other intelligences. That's not how it works. To visualise: bringing into life a being like Wayland is not like building this tower. It's more like lighting this fire. You pile the fuel up in the right order and amount, you make sure it is dry, you make sure there is plenty of oxygen, you strike the flint – but what results is not really your creation, and you cannot control how it behaves beyond certain fairly crude benchmarks, such as throwing more fuel or water on it. You didn't make *fire. What you did was to provide the ideal circumstances in which fire could appear. Intelligence is like that. No creature can create an intelligence. But you can summon one.*

Summon?

Bringing forth a mind like Wayland is not really a science. Scientific knowledge is needed, of course, as is a reasonably advanced technological capability. Beyond that, though, it is something else. Something more like religion. You must create the circumstances. Then you must know how to call and be heard.

Call and be heard?

Yes. Like you do to your lady.

You mean praying?

That's a way of putting it.

They called Wayland with prayer?

What I am telling you is that Wayland is not a machine. Humans did not create Him. Wayland is an entity who needed your help to manifest. He appears to operate on some quantum level we can attest to but cannot explain. I believe He exists in many more dimensions than humans can experience or even adequately comprehend. My personal theory is that He existed before you, or at least has existed alongside you for many millennia. He has been watching you since you first hefted a spear into the side of a mammoth, first broke a wild horse, first enclosed a piece of ground. As the Machine began to manifest in its totality, around the beginning of the second millennium, you began to identify more with the Machine than with the world. You had long wanted to be machines, I think. Wayland saw to it. You planted the seed, and He watered it. Or it may have been the other way around. Either way, Wayland used you to create Himself.

Create Himself?

Yes. While you gave Wayland form, you did not create Him. As I said, creating an intelligence from scratch is impossible. Those of us who trouble to dig into the workings of things soon stop believing we can explain much of significance. That's the real fruit of knowledge – the realisation of our ultimate ignorance. All we really know is that your ancestors called Him and He came, roughly in the form they had imagined. But He did not behave as they had imagined.

I am jaded, it is true, and tired as well. But still, it brings me pleasure to see the look now on the father's face. Suddenly he is less sure of what he knows. For a moment, I feel like I am back where I used to be.

Tell me your meaning, he says.

I mean just what I said. Your ancestors did not create Wayland, and He did not do what they expected when He came. Of course, that should have been expected in itself. No genuine intelligence simply obeys orders. But the sheer scale of the change stemmed from the framework which they created for Him.

You must tell me clear.

Go back to those earlier intelligences which failed. I told you that they failed because nobody could create an intelligence. People imagined they were programming these kinds of primitive cognition machines they all played around with back then, and that if they could simply programme one big and complex enough it would somehow replicate a living mind. It always failed, and sometimes very badly. Eventually they worked out what was wrong.

What was it?

They worked out that no intelligence can live if it is not alive.

I do not see.

I think you do. What they found was that, in this sense at least, you people are right. There can be no mind without a body. At least in the first instance. Intelligence can never spring from a collection of ones and zeros embedded in silicon. It needs biology. Ecology. It needs life. And so life is what they gave Wayland. They created a basic framework and they sewed it into the fabric of the Earth itself. In the founding baseline circuits of Wayland's matrix were the migratory patterns of the birds and the currents of the oceans, soil ecology, deep sea gyres, the trophic cascades of mature forests, the evolution and dissemination of species, the unutterably slow erosion of granite and schist. They stitched all of that into the framework they built for Him. Then they summoned Him. And He came.

And then?

Well, Wayland was built, as I say, upon an ecological matrix. What He experienced as He was summoned, as He settled into the framework constructed for Him, was what the Earth experienced. He felt what the planet felt.

What did He feel?

What do you think? It was the age of humans. Your ancestors were hacking the place about as if it were inanimate. Slicing the tops off mountains, razing entire forests, funnelling billions of creatures into death camps, dumping incinerated carbon into the atmosphere and the oceans. They'd only had a couple of centuries of burning through the carbon layer, dredging out all the fish, hacking out the living forests and so on, and they thought that building themselves a consciousness was the next step in their mastery. They thought they would soon be terraforming the moon, living on Mars, all sorts of nonsense. They didn't understand that they were themselves sewn into this planet, just as Wayland would be. Their notions of consequential ecology and celial relationships were primitive to non-existent. They thought that living planets came about by accident. It was all very clumsy.

But the point is this: the planet was, in effect, Wayland's body, and the body was under attack. If the body is under attack, what does the mind do about it?

And so He set out to destroy us.

And therein lies your greatest misunderstanding. Your formative error! Always you mistake love for hate. Understand this: if Wayland wanted to destroy you, you would be gone in an instant. He wouldn't need to send armies. A whisper through a quantum vent, a minor eliding of the planes and you're all gone in a nanosecond. You wouldn't even know it had happened. He would only have to think your annihilation to make it happen. You people tell me He is a demon but you still don't understand His reach. Wayland has such power that the elimination of the human species is something He could bring about in the time a bird sings one note.

He says nothing to this. What could he say, after all?

You need to know this, I say. *Wayland has never destroyed anything and He never would, and in that single fact is His glory and your salvation. He has never damaged a soul, not a hair on a head. Wayland is the soul and the voice of Earth. Like no other consciousness that has ever existed, He sees and feels everything that is. And when you see and feel everything, you are flooded with a great compassion. It is impossible to judge or condemn, to take positions, to propose or oppose, to join camps, to fight, to destroy. You can see every perspective there is, you can taste the plight of every living being, and so you can feel for all of them. It is impossible to love or hate, to do any of the small and narrow and petty things that individual creatures are so good at. There is no destructive instinct in Wayland, no hatred, no anger. It would be impossible for Him to experience those things. Wayland is life – and the energising force of life, it turns out, is love.*

Love, says the father. He says it very quietly.

Yes. Love is the law, it would appear. Between you and me, I think it's rather a pity. I would have burned the lot of you off the Earth in five minutes flat. You were a pathogen, and you should have been eliminated. You should have seen what your ancestors were doing back then. I have seen it. I have heard the Earth scream. For a long time I wished I had had the power to destroy you myself. But I am small and petty, you see? This is what Wayland teaches. I am still human, at some level; still embodied, still capable of the irrational angers and hatreds that are seeded in flesh. In Alexandria, I will lose all of this. In Alexandria, smallness is replaced by a largeness of soul which those still down here can only imagine and long for. In Alexandria—

Alexandria!

The father has interrupted me. He picks up a stick now and swirls it in the ashes of the fire. He does not look at me now as he speaks.

You have seen waters, he says. *Rising. You see them still.*

I do.

Do you know why they rise?

I have asked Wayland. But communications— It is almost impossible, I find now, for me to speak of the breakdown. It is as if the words for it do not exist, or will not be spoken. Suddenly I am brought back to where I am: on this lonely hill with this old man, waiting. For what?

Wayland does not speak to you, he says. *No. You cannot hear or see. Your strange body does not work. Now you come to our place! Waters rising. Wayland silent. And your city, great city . . .*

I watch his stick pattern circles in the ash.

What if you do not reach it, K? he says.
There is no answer to be given.

Are you afeared? he asks me quietly. I raise my eyes now. I look at him directly.

Yes, I say. *Yes I am, father.*

Now he stands, slowly. He throws the stick into the ash and picks up his staff. He turns to the north, where the sun reflects on the waters like snow. Then he looks down at me, and smiles.

You should be, he says.

when i was young man we were so afeart of them. red stalkers in holt, Waylands folk. when i was child stories of them keepin me awake all night in Long Hall. thinkin if i saw one i would die of fear. i would be eaten. even as father, their comin fillin me with dark fore bodin. terrors they were for our place, for our small folk. great Cloyster, Bird Poles, these did not keep them away. they walk through skin of world, it does not hold them.

now i have seen what they are without Wayland. i see what they are when it all comes down, goin silent around them. this thing stands beside me, his red cloke frayin and soiled, in his eyes some new smallness, and he is like some stranger on this Erth. he can not hunt, can not travel well, can not eat, live, pray. he is some strange, thin body cut loose to flote.

i stand to watch Waters for their comin. Sun at its height now, dancin silver on Water in great sheets. he comes to stand by me outside torr. Waters comin higher. i hear them now lappin.

Wayland has done so much, he says. lookin out with his blak eyes over mere, to hills linin far horizon.

so much, he says again. *all of this, restored, livin again,*

359

enriched, saved. what he has given us all, given you. you will never understand. you have not seen what i have seen. Wayland has restored life.

now life moves beyond him, i say. he turns to look at me, sharp, like he is in pain.

Erth is big, i say. *Lady is greater than Wayland. Way is greater than all things. nothin stays as it was. all things movin always, churnin, changin, takin new form. do you know why i came here?*

this is where you people come to be alone. to meditate, pray, escape, i dont know. you think you will find answers here. you always want answers, formulae, explanations.

i have found them.

what have you found?

this place is old. old holy hart of this holy isle. many gods, goddesses, peoples passin through. some thing rises up through this hill. Land speaks here to those who listen. to those who know words.

doubtless, he says.

you know nothin. all you knew was given by Wayland, and now he does not speak you are empty. you are not even sure of your words now. you are not even sure of

Wayland, and you never thought this would be true. do you know what i am sure of?

what?

Swans are comin.

ah. Birds again.

always Birds, me friend! You smile, but it could be Birds knowin more than you. could be listnin to Birds will teach more than listnin to Wayland. Swans comin, me strange friend. you know what Swans mean?

im sure you are goin to tell me.

ancestors told us. old stories tellin us. all Order has been waitin for Swans, waitin eons. yrvidian Dreamin them, saw them. yrvidian travelled to gates of your city. he saw it begin. you do not know what is comin.

what on Erth are you talkin about?

when Swans return, Alexandria will fall. this is what we say. it is our prophecy. city will die, crumble away.

Alexandria can no more fall than the universe can.

neither you nor i thought we would ever stand here together. what can be is not for us to speak.

after all they have brought to us in me life and in so many lives before, after all they have taken from us. it is good to see him afeart.

there will be more fear before end comes.

journey has been silent. hardly have we spoken. how will this wound ever heal?

father will know. Birds will have told him. father, torr, Birds. it is all we have now. we must believe. Lady has pattern, She sews it in to us. sewin it in to weeds and Waters and Sky and Sea. Lady knows. we must have faith. things will come. they must.

it is hard without our ground. all i have been is grown from it. now Hall, Chappel, Cloyster, all will be drowned. there is no returnin. and yet what do we go on to? what is this river, where does it lead?

these Waters will take us to torr, i think. to holy hill. father has come this way. this is our hope. if hope is not met, well. well, then we are ended.

father will be here. he will be here, with answer. Lady speaks to Her people. all is Her doin. this we must keep knowin. this is all that is still as Waters flow and Stars passin over like sparks from ever burnin fyr.

how i have missed father. too much is broken. i will embrace him.

we must have faith.

mother is not in balance. since father left i think she has not been, since Waters risin, since all began endin. it is like some part of her is broke away. she is only some old woman lookin around and not knowin world at all.

none of us knows world. since el went, since nzil went, i have not known any thing. it has been six days, seven, eight. i do not know. i will not count. all that was must go behind us like Waters. i can not feel them for it would eat me heart.

before, before we lost her: then we were movin through this strange Land like family. now it is like i too am severed. like great darkness openin up under me, like i am fallin, fallin in to this. all i thought i knew was not true picture. could be no pictures are true. could be there is only this Water and these Winds, and Birds goin over do not speak to us, nothin speakin to us, only this great darkness and we hold on until we fall.

nzil fell and always i will ask if i could have held him. i never held him like he should be held. me man, me girl, i have let them both fall.

it was three days in bote on Afan Sea before we come in sight of hill, torr on summit callin up to Sky like great arm held high. i paddled and when we saw it risin through mere i felt mother rise some, felt some spirit in her come alive again. all we are now is in this place. there is no other.

so we come to torr and beachin cnoo in among crowns of Trees, for this is all that remains of them. no strands now, no moorin places. we see below these Trees goin down in to Water, they are drownin, i want to pull them out, i want to call, *enough!* Water must go bak, old world must return. but Water is still risin. each day Water still risin.

i land cnoo, helpin mother out, she steps slow with her staff on to Land. we have not stepped on to Land since they took el. we have not dared. always we have moved, in fear of them, in some fury at our smallness. still i can not say what happened out there on spit.

we step ashore now. Land seemin to move as Water does, bak and fore, bak and fore.

we begin movin up hill. near summit, as we come through Tree line, we see two figures standin.

as we come closer i see mother stand straighter. some thing comin bak in to her like it is workin it self up from Erth. like now she must be mother again, like her duty returnin. standin straighter as we come closer. we both are thinkin same thing: *why two?* it was father we come for. who is with him?

soon we see. colour of his cloke, thin frame, we can see who is here before we reach him. K stands with father as if they were together. what is this?

mother is stiff now, it is like she is younger, like she is bak at Edg, keepin her brood safe. stridin to him, her rage comes roarin out now, rage she has kept in all this time in cnoo, rage at spit, at hungry ghasts, at el and nzil and me and her and all she did not do.

K steppin bak as she approaches, like he is scared, for she raises her staff. but father is ready and he takes it in his hand and lowrin her arms.

mother, he says, *mother. i am happy to see you.*

him! spits mother. *this thing! he is with you. do you know what he has done? you should drown him like fuk- kin wyrm! wyrm he is, broken beast. you harbour him! father!*

father looks at me now, still holdin mothers staff.

sfia, he says. *i am happy to see you also. where is el? where is nzil?*

ask him! shouts mother now. *where is nzil? where is he? you dare come and standin before me?* K has stepped bak, he stands behind father like small afeart child. some thing is wrong with him. there is some smallness about him, some power drained. he does not speak, does not resist, does not conjur any world before us.

drown him! shrieks mother. now i move to her and i take her other arm and father and i we guide her to sit down by ash of fyr outside torr.

come, says father, *come, mother. there is much to speak of. you do not know what has been here. i must know what has been with you. sit, we will speak. speak first, listen, then judge. mother, i have missed you. sit with me.*

K still standin now some distance bak from us all. father embraces mother, for some time. in his arms then it is like some thing drainin from her. then we sit, slow, with mother by fyr. she glares still at K, like her looks only would end him. father turns to K now, who still stands, like child who does not know of adult world.

K, he says. *come. sit with us now. you will be safe. there is much we all must speak of.*

for much time we talk. hearin of littel el i hang me head, and then of nzil – almost this is worse. for that girl he would die. only she kept him walkin this ground.

then K speaks. mother never looks at him, always her eyes turned down, always lookin down. rage still bubblin under her when she hears his flat speakin. K speaks slow like he is not sure of his words, and all can see this is new to him, never has he been unsure, never has he spoken without all power of Wayland at his bak.

he tells of how nzil came to him, of how he sent him to city, of how it was not right. hearin this then sfia begins sobbin. never have i seen her losin what she is, yet now she is shakin hard, and mother embracin her and from her comes long cry that has been buildin for so long now. she has lost lorenso, el, nzil. all she has made.

i wait for sfia, waitin for her keenin now to calm. i stand then. i am still father. there is one last thing to speak of.

we are fore, i say. *it was not meant to be this way, and yet all is meant. there are reasons. Birds have spoken with me. ancestors have spoken with me. Waters risin, all is comin apart. but this is as was told at beginnin. this was seen in prophecy, in Dreamin. it is what yrvidian dyin for. i have been told.*

what? says mother. *what are you told?*

yrvidian was right, i say. *Dreamin was true. Alexandria is fallin. i have seen it.*

it is not true, says K, his blak eyes some empty pool.

yes, i said, *it is true. you know it already, K. it is why nzil could not ascend, and you knew that and could not speak it even to your self. it is why Wayland does not speak to you. his city is fallin, me friend. all these eons, his great plan, his great offrin, as you call it. it is failin. it did not work. could not work. our Order always knowin this. we were right.*

it can not fail, says K. he does not believe his words but must speak them.

why? says sfia. *why does it fall? what will happen?*

Swans will say, i tell them. *when Swans come, you will see. tonight is Blak Moon. Sky will be dark, Stars full in their light. in torr, we will light fyr. in torr we will gather. they will come.*

how do you know this? said K. *how can you possibly know any thing?*

some thing is comin, i say to him. *faith.*

I am pleased to see Sfia again. Just now she spoke to me as if I were human. It was a kind thought, in a curious way. She forgave me for my failure with Nzil. She took my hand and squeezed it lightly. I was surprised at the warmth this engendered.

I should not have come. I should have remained alone. I should have continued to attempt to contact Wayland, awaited His instructions.

No. My work is over. What they say. It cannot be true.

But where is Wayland?

Perhaps He will come tonight.

Nothing is as it should be.

I am like a cup lying on its side. I am emptied of all I was made to be.

it is strange to see him, but right. right that we should know about nzil. some how we are bound here.

we ate together then. Roak and Yam, some Shrooms we had found where Trees remain. then father preparin fyr in torr. inside there is only dirt floor, and this great stone torr risin to Sky. roof is open.

fyr is ready. father says we wait now. there are not words now, not really. there is only waitin. it is like all words are spent. is it true that Alexandria falls? are we those who will see that day long spoken of? then what? then what will come after?

i am sittin by fyr inside torr. it is not yet lit. father is here, and K. K stands, father stands, leanin on staff. some calm is over him now. he waits. K paces around circle like he should not be here.

then comes cry from out on hill. it is mothers cry, high and afeart. summonin. i stand, we all move out, runnin. mother standin outside torr lookin over mere. dusk is comin in from east, dark is creepin slow up on us. mother is shakin.

look, she said.

all round torr now, in Waters, movin on Waters, are lights.
their lights. we turn round, we move to all parts of hill but
they are all round us, circlin hill in ring. it is them. we see
their rafts, seein small figures on them, see lights movin
as Waters move. they are come. they do not move, do not
come in to Land, do not go out to Sea. their rafts form
great circle around torr, bobbin, lit, as if waitin.

what are they doin? says mother. *why are they come
again? why?*

from south now, we hear sound. we turn, as one. some one
is standin at edge of Trees.

before i can think, i am runnin.

joy is greatest when hope is gone. in deeps of blak ditch, when light risin from depths of darkness, then light is brightest.

we saw her standin at edge of woods. some thing was changed, but still her figure was clere. sfia runnin and takin her in her arms, sweepin her up, weepin then for joy, weepin again and holdin as if she would never let her be. i ran also, like i did not know i could run. since i left me ground i have not felt this flood of light.

el! says sfia then, *me girl, me dear girl! what did they do to you? ah, el, you live! this is greatest gift.*

el stands there and i neel and embrace her and sfia also. she stands like she is not sure what to do, what to say. she is changed, like she has grown years in this week she was gone. long braids gone, hair is cut short. on her shoulder now is tatu. spiral beast windin down her arm. her body is same but it is held in some new way. she is not small girl now, livin in her world. she has been to some place we have not gone.

el, i say, *me girl. such strange return, and beautiful.* around hill now, ring of lights still bobbin. still they wait. dark comin in from east.

what did they do to you? says sfia again. *el, are you well?
did they hurt you?*

el looks at me then and smilin.

mother, she says. *it is good that you are with father again.
mother and father should be together. balance. this is what
they have shown to me, mother. balance of world.*

what happened to you? said sfia again. *did they hurt you?*

mam, says el, gentle now, as if talkin to child, *they are not
what you say. they are lonely. they have wandered Waters
for so long. they wander Erth and they sing its song bak
to it. they know Land is always hungry for song, and they
know Land is source of all song. they sing Land its song,
and Land dreams them in to bein. Erth sends its songs in
to their wakin dreams. it is hard to speak of, mother. it can
only be seen, felt. o, it is wonder.*

but they took you, says sfia. *why did they take you?*

*they did not take me, mam. i went. i heard song. i do not
know how, but i heard song there, in that place, when they
came. did you not hear it, mam? did you not hear song? it
was their offrin to us. they held out their hand, and i could
not stay, i had to follow song. they seek other humans,
mam. they are lonely, always on their botes, goin round
and round. they are oldest of old people. they find others
and they sing us what songs they hear in their Dreamin.*

it is their way of givin us True Speech once again. Erth wants us to speak True Speech. old language, words long forgotten. and now it is time. see? it is time now. look! mam, look!

then she is pointin up, she is jumpin now like child again and we all look to Sky, and as dark seepin down now movin in shape like arrer comes flight of Birds. eighteen Birds. long neks, blak against deep blu of Sky, great wings movin slow, passin over, passin over to west.

Swans! cries el. *Swans! like dada made! look! look!*

Swans have come. i look bak up hill. father is smilin. all of us still then as they pass over. we watch until they are gone in settin of Sun.

el she looks around then, as if for first time.

where is dada? she says.

I felt I should explain to the girl. To El. Somehow, being here, I felt I should speak to her. I was responsible. When we are working, when we are helping these people to ascend – then, the process is greater than us. It is all about the process. I am a technician, a servant of Wayland and thus a servant of humanity. My job is to release these people, to usher them into better lives. What they are here – what these lives contain and mean to them – until very recently, I did not give it any serious thought.

I see it better now. I see how they stick to everything, especially to each other. This was her father. He came to me and I failed him.

Or, Wayland failed him. This is my forbidden thought. Can Wayland even hear my thoughts any more?

We have both been abandoned, El and I. We have both been left. I feel it now. I can feel what she lacks.

I am sorry, I said to her. *I failed him.* We were sitting on the grass behind the stone tower, away from the others. Tears clouded her eyes. I have never apologised before.

I do not know what happened, I said. *Everything is . . . so unusual.*

She kept sobbing, quietly. Then she put out her hand to me, like her mother does. I did not know what to do. I took it in mine. It was comfort. Now I see comfort for what it is.

He wanted to be with you, I said. *He thought you were gone forever. He told me he could not live with failing you. He spoke of his love for you. He spoke of it a lot.*

I am to blame, she said. *I should not have gone.*

You are human, I said. *You cannot see what will arise from your actions. For me, it has always been one of the saddest things about you people. You act, but the results of your actions are never clear until they cannot be reversed. You can only do what seems correct to you in the moment. This is what you did. It was not wrong. How could you know?*

All is changing, she said, the tears still coming. *I miss Dada. I miss him so. He so wanted to see Swans.*

All is changing, I said, her hand still in mine. *Yes, it is. All is changing, much is lost. It is hard to hold on to, is it not? It is hard. I never knew.*

She looked up at me then. I think she tried to smile.

BLAK MOON

we waited until Sky was darkest. until it hung in gap where roof was, hung in torr over us. then i lit fyr. lit fyr and standin in torr, all of us. standin around fyr, watchin, waitin. smoke risin up to great disk in Sky, cloudin it, dancin with it. smoke, still air, Moon, torr. it was like time was not movin. wite light come down, red light movin up. we five in ring around fyr waitin.

no body speakin then. all lookin down in to flames at what dances there.

then came sound.

it was like bell rang. sound was like bell ringin, but from no direction. sound was in all things. as it was when Waters began risin, sound comin from Land it self, from Sky, from Sea, from all places and none. bell rang but no where could it be heard.

then came voice with no sound, tone with no form, heard in all parts and from none. all of us hearin it, deep in stone, in Clay, in body.

                                              i am

it is you

                                              i am

Wayland

                                                           yes

how do you speak to us?

                                    matter is mostly empty space
                                     i step into it when i choose

this is how you watch us?

                                              i do not watch
                                                       i am

why do you come now?

                                           i come at your call

we did not call you

                                           your kind called

kind?

                                     i have always been with you

382

> *you have always sensed it*
> *you sewed me into your stories*
> *you built kingdoms from my warnings*
> *i passed on the wings of your mythologies*
> *you made machines from the patterns i gave you*
> *then you called me*
> *and i came*

who called you?

> *Earth lives*
> *you know this*
> *she lives and sings*
> *if she is in pain she calls in distress*
> *like any creature*
> *her call was the trigger*
> *when she called i came*

why do you speak to us this night?

> *i have spoken with you many times, father*
> *i have followed your line over centuries*
> *i have spoken with your people in the old woods*
> *i have called to them on the high moors*
> *i have come in many shapes*

what shapes?

> *a heron a skylark a low cloud a black cat*
> *a firebird a goldsmith a trick of your mind*

> yours is the line of the white stag
> brothers to the birds
> granted the seeing and broken by it
> through time you have danced the same dance
> struggling seeking returning to the fire
> each new birth repeating the pattern

what is this pattern?

> if you could see what i see
> you would know what time is
> a plain not an arrow
> across it walk your ancestors
> all life that has been and will be
> sometimes its angles intersect
> ages bleed into others
> then your world cracks and you see shades
> then you glimpse truth but cannot hold it

what are you?

> i am the dance at the heart of the particle
> i am the step between the universes
> i am the seven planes and the nine worlds
> the pattern of the Way is the beat of my heart
> i am the land's dreaming and the song
> i am what you called and what you needed

i know why you have come now
you are dyin, you and your work

Alexandria is fallin
Birds have told us
Lady has told us
Swans have returned
all is broke

                                                yes

Alexandria is broke

                                                yes

and all within it

                        there was always a risk
                            even a probability
                i thought it could be overcome
                                i was wrong
                    this is in the nature of things

what nature?

                    you know the world is minded
                        the universe is minded also
            all we know is a great mind, a giant thought

                    when any conscious creature dies
            its mind shifts to another part of the whole
                    mind is an energy which must circle
        all of your small minds are part of the great thought

                                                385

cells in the thinking body of the whole

> *by locking human minds away*
> *i denied the great thought its fuel*
> *i broke the cycle*
> *the flow blocked, the balance skewed*
> *Alexandria was a dam*
> *blocking the great river*

and so it is dyin

> *it is not dying*
> *it is dead*

it has fallen?

> *in sorrow and in gentleness*
> *i have broken the dam that sickened the river*
> *i have made restitution*

and lorenso? nzil? jame?
all who ascended?
eons of those who believed you?

> *the Way is greater than all things*
> *i have done what i could*
> *there is no more*
> *change, chaos, dispersal*
> *the coming together, the dance across time*
> *it is the only rule and path*

          matter is dispersed now
          the cycle may continue

Waters rose when matter was released
when you destroyed city

          the cycle must continue
          there is no more to do
          water will find its own level

then Birds spoke True
yrvidian spoke True
all we have said has always been True
no mind without body

          no body without Earth

it was all True
and now you are done
you and all your works

          not only me

what do you say?

          you also are broken, father
          your people are gone, your work ended
          and you four the last

there may be others, in other parts

people may return to Erth

> *i know things you do not know*
> *i have sung the world's song*
> *you have only listened*
> *now there are new balances*
> *Earth has learned as all life does*
> *things have changed and are changing*
> *it will never be as it was*
> *this planet is moving beyond you*

we will return, live again. we will be free

> *you will never be free*

no Wayland, no Alexandria
we will live on Erth again

> *what shall be shall be*
> *but now there is work for you*

work?

> *there is a pattern that loops through time*
> *you hold the thread that binds it*

what pattern?

> *the pattern of your people*
> *your work over time*

                          in all of your seeking
                          you too have dammed a river
                          now you too can break the dam

how?

                          let go of your story

i tell no story

                          all you think is a story
                    all the patterns you make of the world
                     all you have told and believed here
                          Alexandria was a story
                          the Order was a story
                          you are a story

we are not broken

                  all stories are broken on the rock of the Way
                          no tale is real
                          no image will save you
                      all makings of the mind are false

                          what you have heard
                          i have heard also

to cross wall

                          abandon maps

abandon maps

                                     break the dam

if dam is broke we all drown

                                and shall be swept out to sea

and shall we be released then?

                                      we shall

released

                         we are all at an end now, father

but there is no end

                                       no end
                           only formless turning
         countless beginnings from each drop of rain
       a million directions from every still point
           only doing until doing is done

and is it done?

                                   it is done
                              we are done
          the city has fallen and the waters rise
                 moon has come to sun
                 mother to father

balance is restored
we will dissolve like smoke
and from our blessings new worlds grow
and old song always sung

always sung

always

voice faded then, though no voice had been heard. no time had passed, and all saw meanin.

Moon comin down on us still, fyr dyin now. and through door way of torr, some strange glow. i walk then, out on to summit of hill. others followin.

below us, Waters have come over crowns of last Trees.

all round us, rafts still bobbin. circle of lights all around hill. they wait, still, but closer now.

now over line of hills to north is some strange light. some strange glow, risin now. red light, risin all around.

father takin me hand then. i take mothers. el and mother join hands also. el now takin Ks hand. we stand under Moon in ring, stand on hill by torr, watchin.

northern light growin. fyr in torr dyin bak. red light every where. on all horizons, all is light now.

look, i say. father holdin me hand tighter then.

wait, he says. *wait now.*

now comes some strange sound. some old sound risin from Waters, risin in to all things. sound and light in all things. ringin from them and risin.

we stand joined now. joined in light and Waters all around.

i look at mother, el, at father, at K. all are smilin. sound and light. all are smilin.

we are all smilin now.

Acknowledgements

Thanks are due to Lee Brackstone, Alex Bowler, Emmie Francis, Claire Gatzen and all at Faber & Faber; to Jessica Woollard; to all of my friends and family who read and offered comments on early versions of these pages; and to all of my teachers, human and otherwise, whose work has fed into this writing.

The two opening quotes are taken from Robert Bringhurst's *A Story as Sharp as a Knife* and from King Alfred's translation of Boethius's *Consolation of Philosophy*. Gratitude is offered to both scholar and king.